And I Love You So

And I Love You So

A Story of Love and Loss

Melanie Baker Trimarco

Foreword by Genevieve V. Georget

Copyright 2020 Melanie Baker Trimarco

All rights reserved. Except as permitted under the
US Copyright Act of 1976, no part of this publication may
be reproduced, distributed, or transmitted in any form or
by any means, or stored in a database or retrieval system,
without the prior written permission of the publisher.

 Writers of the Round Table Press
PO Box 1603, Deerfield, IL 60015
www.roundtablecompanies.com

Editor: **Genevieve Georget**
Cover Designer: **Sunny DiMartino**
Illustrator: **Sunny DiMartino**
Interior Designer: **Christy Bui**
Proofreaders: **Adam Lawrence, Carly Cohen**

Printed in the United States of America

First Edition: May 19, 2020
10 9 8 7 6 5 4 3 2 1

Library of Congress Cataloging-in-Publication Data
Baker Trimarco, Melanie.
And I love you so / Melanie Baker Trimarco.—1st ed. p. cm.
ISBN Paperback: 978-1-61066-082-2
ISBN Digital: 978-1-61066-083-9
Library of Congress Control Number: 2020905108

Writers of the Round Table Press and the logo
are trademarks of Writers of the Round Table, Inc.

Minor adjustments for punctuation and grammar have been
made to communication exchanges and journal entries.

For my Sweetheart, Mark, my kind, gentle Love who always saw the best in us.

For our parents and families, who supported us through the wonderful and the most difficult times.

Foreword

I ONCE WENT ON VACATION WITH a group of women I had never met. We flew in from every edge of the continent and found ourselves sitting around a large wooden table, with the warm Caribbean air gently blowing through the room.

We were about to spend the week going on a journey together that extended from the ocean to the jungle. We would visit mountains and villages and island life from a different perspective.

But more importantly, we would discover a side of ourselves that we had never seen before. Because when we bring others into our story, we also bring life to that story. And those stories begin to shape us and guide us and, most beautiful of all, they heal us.

The first time that Melanie and I sat on the phone together, a stillness filled the air between us.

Not a discomfort or an awkwardness ... but a serenity. A moment to breathe in the journey that we were about to take together. It wasn't going to be a journey through mountains or far-off villages, but rather a journey into the deepest parts of her pain and vastest parts of her faith.

It was going to be the journey of bringing her story of love and loss into a world that so desperately needed to hear it.

But first, it was going to be a journey of living through it all over again.

Because that's what writing this kind of book really is: it's about returning to the darkest corners and sitting gratefully in the brightest light and making it all real again.

Which isn't an easy thing to do when your story includes sitting next to the man you love as he takes his last breath.

But as I learned while walking this road alongside Melanie, this story is about more than her own grief and growth. This story is very much about standing alongside others as they go through the same thing. This story is about a desire to reach out across the page and make someone else—anyone else—feel a little less alone as they endure the hardest goodbye of their life.

It's a story about hurting and healing . . . together.

It has been an immense privilege watching Melanie bring this book to life. To stand with her as she endured the raw discomfort of putting words to her experience and meaning to her pain.

And I Love You So is a book that was not only created out of great love for her own story, but out of love for the story you may be living as well.

And any story written out of love . . . is a story worth receiving with love.

May you feel the grief, may you find hope in the beauty, may you rise through the courage.

May you allow Melanie's story to give wings to your own.

With love,
Genevieve Georget

When you go through deep waters
I will be with you.

Isa. 43:2 (New Living Version)

The Final Farewell

Mark took his last breath at 8:06 p.m. on October 9, 2017, with my mom, my dad, and me in our bedroom. I phoned his parents to let them know Mark went to Heaven. I still remember how his mom said, "NOOOOOO." They came over to say goodbye. The hospice nurse arrived shortly after; she was an angel, so sweet and caring, and she explained every single detail of what was going to happen until the time Mark's body was taken away from our home to the funeral home. She told me we would need to dispose of all of Mark's medications and arrange for medical services to retrieve the equipment, and then informed me about what would happen when the funeral director arrived. She contacted the funeral home, and they promptly arrived at our home.

When the white, windowless van pulled up in my dark driveway, I think I tapped into some sort of superpower to keep it together. I knew I needed to maintain my dignity, but inside I wanted to scream from the top of my lungs. I could not believe this was really happening—that Mark's body was being taken from the home that we both loved, and that his body would never be present here again. It was so final.

Despite his lengthy illness, I never really focused on this moment. The end. The end of our lives together on this Earth. The moment when my Sweetheart would not be by my side. It was over.

His pain.

His suffering.

His dependence on me to care for his every need.

Our union.

I couldn't process the magnitude of this moment; I was hollow inside. I could only ask God to keep me intact. I asked Him to bathe me with grace and necessary strength to be a good wife for my husband one final time.

I greeted the two gentlemen from the funeral home and invited them in. They were so kind and compassionate and assured me they would take great care of my Love. I wanted to know exactly where they were taking my husband. I asked if I could be with them as they took Mark away. The director gently told me it was completely up to me if that is what I wanted to do. He explained this may be something I felt I wanted to do, and it was important to know that this would be my last memory of him. Wow! I quickly played the scene in my head and knew this would not be the right move for me. I wanted my last memory of Mark in our home to be the peaceful look on his face after he took his last breath.

I asked if I could look inside the van so I could see exactly where they were taking him. We walked down the lit walkway into the cool fall night air, they opened the van, and I peered inside of the big dark empty space awaiting my beloved. Hard to believe this was happening. I walked back inside while they went into our bedroom to prepare for his departure. I joined the hospice nurse at the kitchen table to finish up accounting for the disposal of all his medications. Dad came over to let me know Mark would be leaving. Mom came with me into the laundry room so my view of his departure would be completely blocked. I just couldn't bear to witness Mark's dead body leaving our home.

Who would have known that our marriage would only last for fifteen years and four days? Who would have known on our wedding day, as we recited our vow to love in sickness and in health, that we would start loving in sickness in 2008? How could we even imagine that we would love till death do us part on October 9, 2017?

How many couples really think about the depth of the vows they are preparing to recite as bride- and groom-to-be? How many allow themselves to go to the dark side of that commitment to love for worse, for poorer, and in sickness fully understanding the meaning without a frame of reference?

We did not. We pictured ourselves growing old together. We understood the meaning of the words within the vows. We knew marriage was work and required nurturing and there would be good and bad times, but didn't think the death part would happen so soon. You never think you are going to be the exception.

But we were.

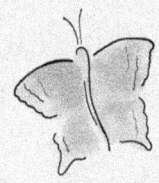

Ask and it will be given to you; seek and you will find; knock and the door will be opened to you.

Matt. 7:7
(New International Version)

The Man I Met Who Would Become My Husband

I GRADUATED FROM THE UNIVERSITY OF Southern Mississippi in December of 1990 with a bachelor of science degree in hospitality, restaurant, and tourism management. I was the girl who couldn't figure out what she wanted to do with her life. I began college the summer after high school graduation; looking back, I should have taken the break. Over the course of the next few years, I grappled with finding the right academic path for me. I went from journalism to business to nursing, and finally landed on hospitality. I always loved party planning and organizing, and thought this would be the right major for me to pursue. I loved it!

Shortly after graduation, I moved back home to New Orleans to begin my job search. I searched the classified ads in the *Times-Picayune* newspaper every Sunday, trying to find a job to begin building my career. As I was in the career-search mode, I began working as a cocktail server and then a bartender on the *Creole Queen*—a boat built in 1983 modeled after paddle wheelers from the 1850s. I worked the dinner cruise shift, and every night felt like a party! The mood was quite festive as tourists dined on delicious gumbo, seafood, and other local fare. Entertainment was provided by a jazz trio as guests danced the evening away or relaxed while sipping a Sazerac, a rye whiskey cocktail invented locally in the 1800s.

I had a few interviews here and there—some local, one in Meridian, Mississippi, and another in Pensacola, Florida—but nothing really suited me. After about five months of bartending, although fun and great cash, it was time for me to focus on my job search to find that place where I could launch a career. I happened to see an ad in the Sunday classified section of the newspaper. A major hotel company was seeking a food and beverage director, so I applied. Deep down, I knew I did not have the qualifications for such a role but decided to take a chance.

I received a call for an interview! I was excited about the possibility of beginning a position in my field of study. Since I did not have the necessary experience for a director role, I interviewed for a food and beverage supervisor, an entry-level supervisory role. I went through the interview process and then learned the job was based in Tulsa, Oklahoma. I was offered the position along with a wage of $7.50 per hour, with guaranteed overtime. Without hesitation, I jumped in with both feet and moved to a state I never visited and where I knew no one. Not. A. Single. Person.

A bit nervous but excited, I packed up and drove to Tulsa with a girlfriend and started my adventure. We took turns driving the 685 miles from the New Orleans area and had lots of laughs along the way. This was one of nine moves I made during my early college and career days. As I look back, I know this forced me to be the independent person I am today, and helped build my core strength for anything that would come my way in the future.

I lived in the hotel for the first few weeks while looking for an apartment. This was my first time living solo, and I was excited for this next chapter. My parents and brother drove a U-Haul with my belongings and helped me to get settled. It was perfect!

After about nine months, I was promoted to an assistant

manager and transferred back to New Orleans. I thrived in learning management skills and was eager to climb the career ladder in my profession. I worked very hard and did what I needed to do to make a difference and achieve the goals I set out to accomplish.

After spending eighteen months in New Orleans, I was ready for the next position up. There was not an opportunity at the hotel in New Orleans. A former colleague connected me with an opportunity at a resort on the Mississippi Gulf Coast as a restaurant general manager for an iconic seafood restaurant right on the water. After my interview, I was offered a position and accepted. I loved moving to Biloxi, Mississippi. I loved the view of the Gulf of Mexico and the sandy beaches. I was only about ninety miles from my family and hometown, so I was able to visit often. My stint at this resort was very short-lived as my supervisor was a jerk. He would sit behind his big desk and bark orders. He had no people skills, was condescending, and was not interested in two-way conversations. I wasn't interested in working in such a poor environment.

The gaming industry was taking off on the Gulf Coast, and I accepted a restaurant general manager position for a casino that was under construction. This was my launching pad for my career. I learned quickly and had great success with managing my restaurant. I began mentoring other managers and then became part of the new restaurant opening team as other casinos were being built in Louisiana, Mississippi, and Las Vegas. I was promoted to a training manager and relocated to Plymouth, Minnesota, for eighteen months, and was then transferred back to the Mississippi Gulf Coast.

In January of 2000, I accepted a role with a growing restaurant chain and landed in Manhattan, New York. I was thrilled and excited to be in the Big Apple. My first day in Manhattan, I went to Starbucks to be in a familiar environment, and that is where this Southern girl got her wake-up call—and it wasn't the coffee! I ordered a cappuccino from the barista, and she shouted, "stay or go?!" Startled, I asked her to repeat what she said. Again, she barked, "Stay or go?!" I quickly learned this was the Manhattan way to say, "Would you like your cappuccino for here or to go?" Ha! I felt like a fish out of water. I quickly adapted to the fast pace; my morning commute on the subway felt like a traffic jam, but instead of cars, the jam was caused by people.

I lived right on the corner of Fifty-Fourth and Second in the middle of Midtown Manhattan, and to top it off, the company paid my rent. After about nine months, I was relocated to corporate headquarters based in Chicago, IL. I fell in love with Chicago—it was a smaller and cleaner version of Manhattan to me. I rented a beautiful condominium in River North with a doorman, grocery store, and a restaurant in my building. I enjoyed Michigan Avenue as my backyard.

Michigan Avenue is also known as "The Magnificent Mile" and is an upscale area with beautiful architecture, luxury retailers (great for window shopping), the best restaurants, and spectacular landscaping reflective of the season. There was always a festival, celebration, nearby theatre, and a mecca for people-watching!

At the time, I was on the road weeks upon weeks for my job, as we were opening new restaurants on both coasts. I lived in hotels and would dash home for a quick weekend to pay bills—before the age of e-bills! While I thoroughly enjoyed my career, I had a life that did not allow for settling down or for finding someone to share it with.

By this point in my life, I was ready to find my one and only. But how? I traveled a ton, and my friends were coworkers. I had dated over the years and, outside of my first love, did not have a long-term relationship. As I settled into my new life in downtown Chicago, I decided to place an ad on Match.com. It felt a bit strange shopping for a date on the internet since it was a nontraditional way to find a date! What if the person on the other end wasn't who he said he was? Was he into playing games, and how would I sift through the nonsense? Additionally, this was the very early days of internet dating sites. However, I was ready for more than the career I had; I was ready to share the life I was building with someone and not be alone. At thirty-five years old, I was pretty settled in my routines and was quite independent. The moves to different places over the years instilled reliance on me, and me alone. I was a bit nervous, maybe scared, but I was ready.

I created my profile describing my ideal person, and shared my likes and interests. Shortly after I created my profile, I had a few men who were interested. There was one guy, Mark, who was great. We hung out, went to dinner, and explored the city together.

However, we didn't have a real connection, and the experience we shared was mere companionship. We went on dinner dates, went to movies, and enjoyed watching sports at the local pub. But I wanted more than that; I wanted to find my other half, my one and only.

Another Mark entered my world in early 2001. I saw Mark's profile and was immediately drawn to his smile and his profile. I liked what I read and really liked the specificity of his profile. I liked that it was clear he knew what he was looking for. It seemed like he was ready to settle down. I was too.

This six-foot-five man, who enjoyed the movies, travel, dancing, dining, and romancing, described himself as "just a guy, who has been out there, looking for someone who is family-oriented, and not carrying a world of emotions and problems on her shoulders. I am ready for something serious, have been for a long time. I just want to find the same thing in a woman; please no game players or someone looking to fill a gap temporarily. I have not plunged into marriage for one reason—I won't settle for less than someone who I can make happy and who can make me happy, too."

He went on to add, "I am a total romantic, honest, loyal, and sincere. I have stayed single because I would rather wait than to marry the wrong person. I love kids, animals, am very family-oriented, and I would love to start my own family with a very special lady. She must be kind, loving, average build, and come from a good solid background with very little emotional baggage."

We exchanged a few emails and then began speaking on the phone. He seemed like a nice guy . . . a really nice guy. We talked on the phone and emailed several times a day. I so looked forward to our daily exchange.

Due to my work schedule, the majority of my time was spent *away* from Chicago rather than *in* Chicago. We could never find the time to meet in person. He would try to plan a date, but I was either exhausted from traveling or on the road. After a few months of this back-and-forth and never being able to meet, I emailed him to let him know it was best for us to move on. I was just too busy with my life on the road to make time for meeting him. Or so I said via email to him. Honestly, this man seemed too good to be true for me. We got along so well, had similar interests, but I kept waiting for the other shoe to drop. I was falling for this man I never met in person and was scared to let someone in—as much as I wanted that partnership and my one and only. I simply did not want to get hurt. So, I doubted. What if he was a player? What if all of this was fake? He kindly replied via email and wished me well.

A few months went by, but in my heart, I knew I was shortchanging myself. I knew that there was a risk in letting someone in—whether it was Mark or anyone else. I could not continue to hide behind an internet ad, a phone call, or an email. Mark and I clicked from the beginning, so I owed it to myself to meet him in person to see if the rapport, the friendship was genuine. I read through some of our email exchanges and thought about our conversations, and then took a leap of faith on Father's Day, June 17, 2001, and emailed him.

> Hello Mark,
>
> You popped into my mind, and I thought I would say hello.
>
> Hope all is well with you. Are you still searching for your one and only?
>
> If not, I hope you are happy. If so, might I have an opportunity to reenter your world?
>
> A few months ago, you and I were in the getting-to-know-one-another level . . . I felt comfortable with you in conversation, and when it came down to the wire to meet you, I got cold feet. For that, I apologize.
>
> It's funny . . . sometimes the very thing we want in life can be so scary.
>
> Needless to say, I am interested in meeting you and seeing if we actually do click.
>
> If that is something you would be interested in, let me know; if not, I completely understand.
>
> —Melanie

A few hours later I received this email from him:

> Melanie, you may never believe this, but I was thinking about you just last week and, in my heart, hoping I would someday hear from you again. And, yesssssssssssss!!! I want to meet you and see what happens. Right now, it is Father's Day and my brother and I are taking my dad out to play 9 holes of golf.

> Give me your phone number again, and I will call you tomorrow night. Let's set up a time and place to meet. I do miss you, talking; we got along so great. I was very sad when we couldn't meet, but now I am overjoyed :)
>
> Glad you are back!!!!!!!!!!!!!!!!!!!!!!!!
>
> Hugs, Mark

I flew out to DC for work on that Monday. Every single evening, we spent hours on the phone. We continued to get to know each other, but it was in a more intimate way. We shared our stories and our hopes, and let each other into our souls. We talked about having children together, about our families, our careers, our disappointments and dreams. Through the course of those nightly conversations, I fell in love with this man on the telephone.

Sight unseen.

I knew he was the one for me.

He knew I was the one for him.

I fell in love with Mark's voice as that was my only tangible connection. His voice was like that of a radio announcer. Strong, confident, and silky. He projected kindness, and there was a sense of security I felt with him on the phone. We shared an easy banter. Mark spoke from his heart. I knew this man was my other half.

I emailed Mark on Thursday, June 21, and in this email to the man I never met in person, I said I firmly believed God brought us together to love each other for as long as we are on this Earth together. Mark and I loved each other without judgment before we ever laid eyes on one another. This was a union that was supposed to happen—I believe that with every fiber of my being.

Mark offered to pick me up from the airport on that Friday night. I was a bit nervous about this because my logical side kicked in. Yes! I fell in love with him, his voice, his values, but the reality was that I had never met him. What if he was a stalker? What if this wasn't real?

My flight home was scheduled to depart Washington, DC, in the evening. There were storms in the area and all flights were canceled.

I couldn't help but think this was a sign! I began doubting myself a bit. My *Law and Order SVU* side kicked in and took this diversion to a whole different place. What if this man wanted to pick me up from the airport with ill intentions—like kidnapping me and then cutting me up into tiny pieces?

I contacted Mark to let him know of my travel delay, and he offered to pick me up that morning when I arrived. My first, second, and third thoughts were "NO! No way!" I knew the state my face and hair would be in, and I wanted to make a great first in-person impression. I suggested we meet on Saturday evening and invited him to meet me at my downtown condominium, after which we could head to Navy Pier to grab dinner. Navy Pier is one of Chicago's top attractions, with shops, restaurants, and fun things to do. He agreed, and we ended our conversation, looking forward to our first face-to-face encounter.

I arrived early the next morning to get my flight changed. I approached the agent to get my seating assignment, and she quickly informed me there were no more seats. The flight was overbooked due to the previous night's cancelations. I literally placed my head on the counter in despair. I explained that I had been on the road for a week and it was important for me to get home. After what seemed like an eternity, she handed me a ticket. She gave me the last seat on the plane in first class. I was delighted to be heading home, eager to meet this man I wanted to see in person, and took this as a sign that all would be well. I arrived in Chicago, took a taxi home, and prepared for my date.

Mark arrived promptly at our agreed-upon time. There were security cameras in the lobby that fed onto my television. When the doorman buzzed me to let me know I had a visitor, I was able to get a preview! As much as I felt comfortable with the direction this was going, I still had my guard up. Still hoping this man had great intentions! His first impression via security camera seemed normal. I was comfortable letting him come up to my condo, as the doorman was just a quick buzz away if the meeting turned south.

As I waited for him to take the elevator up to my condo, I could hardly contain my excitement! I had butterflies in my stomach but was joyful this moment was finally happening. This was it, the moment of truth! Would those preconceived feelings translate in person? The moments quickly ticked by as I awaited his elevator ride up to my floor. I greeted Mark at the door. He was so very sweet. We immediately embraced and passionately kissed. He brought roses, candy, and the movie video *You've Got Mail*. I remember him twirling me in the foyer. Everything simply felt right. All the pieces of getting to know this man I fell in love with on the telephone came together. His kindness, warmth, the secure feeling I felt with him during our phone conversations materialized in person. A million thoughts besieged me—he was romantic, kind, and good-looking!

As I reflect back on this moment, this is who Mark was. He was kind, thoughtful, and generous. He loved to surprise me and take care of me.

We went to Navy Pier and went to one of his favorite seafood restaurants, Riva. It was a Saturday evening, and we did not have reservations, so Riva was not in the cards for us. Instead, we went to the foot of the pier and ordered counter service—he had an Italian beef sandwich with a Coke, and I had a slice of cheese pizza with a Diet Coke. We talked and talked and talked; it was so fun to be together and so comfortable. He had me home by midnight. He was insistent that we have a "proper dinner date" the following day.

We did.

We were inseparable from that point forward.

My mom and dad arrived from New Orleans for a visit, and I was anxious for them to meet this man I fell in love with. Since this was their first visit, I enjoyed taking them around the city to explore all the beautiful things Chicago had to offer. We went to the top of the Hancock building. This tourist attraction boasts incredible views of the city and Lake Michigan. We were seated in the lounge and ordered cocktails and appetizers. Although I only met Mark *in person* the previous week, I let my parents in on this new man in my life and wanted them to meet him. I told them he was someone I could see spending the rest of my life with.

Of course, Mom wanted to know how we met. When I told her we met through Match.com, an online service, she quickly said not to tell anyone about that part! My mom and dad were skeptical that this man was the right person for me. It certainly was not the traditional way people met one another—especially for their generation. My parents have known each other since they were in grammar school and married in 1960! The concept of meeting your life partner online was completely foreign to them.

They all met.

They all clicked.

It was love at first sight for them too.

Shortly after, I met Mark's mom and dad. Again, we clicked. It was as if this was what the universe wanted. What God wanted.

Mark and I continued to spend every spare moment we had together. We explored the city together, learned about each other—discovered one another. We were so very happy. He and I were both looking for the exact same thing—to find a partner to share our love and life with. Mark was quick-witted, a history buff, and master of all things electronic. Mark was a Chicago native, with an older brother and younger sister. The middle child! He was a banker who enjoyed building relationships with customers, and he enjoyed going out of his way to help them. People always seemed to be drawn to Mark, as it was easy to strike up a conversation with him. He made you feel as if you were the most important person. His brain was like no other—it eventually became my rolodex ... this guy remembered EVERYTHING!

We were engaged exactly two months and one day after we met. We knew that we wanted to get married and spend our lives as one. Mark always liked to surprise me, but he always had a hard time containing the surprise. Over the years, it became a joke. One day we were talking, and he asked what style of ring I wanted, and I told him I was fond of emerald cut. He wanted to get me the perfect engagement ring.

Our engagement took place on the eve of my thirty-sixth birthday at my condo. I knew we were going out but wasn't sure of where—he just told me to wear a dress! Mark arrived at my condo with a lovely bouquet of flowers in hand. We were hanging out, and then he dropped to one knee and asked me to be his wife. Of course, I said YES! We took pics and called our loved ones to share our great news. We celebrated on a boat, the *Odyssey*, and enjoyed a dinner cruise on Lake Michigan. My Love was a romantic at heart.

As I look back on this time in my life, so much of what was going on was really left up to the plan that was carved out for me before I was even born. You see, I prayed for a partner, a lover, and a friend to share my life with. Out of all the men on this Earth, God chose Mark for me. God chose me for Mark.

God knew what was in store for us the moment we connected. God knew Mark and I would not live together to a ripe old age. God knew Mark would encounter illness after illness. God knew I would have the strength to stand by his side.

God knew we needed one another.

*Love is patient, love is kind. It does
not envy, it does not boast, it is not proud.
It does not dishonor others, it is not self-
seeking, it is not easily angered, it keeps no
record of wrongs. Love does not delight in
evil but rejoices with the truth. It always
protects, always trusts, always hopes,
always perseveres. Love never fails.*

1 Cor. 13:4–8 (NIV)

Until Death Do Us Part

In Catholicism, the expectation is for those seeking union in the Church is to participate in marriage preparation class known as Pre-Cana. The goal is to help Catholic couples create a strong foundation for marriage. The name is derived from John 2:1–12 and is based on the wedding feast at Cana where Jesus performed his first public miracle, changing water into wine. Since "pre" means "before," couples prepare for their personal wedding feast and establish the foundation for a long, healthy, and happy marriage with as much, if not more, effort as they apply to planning their wedding day.

We attended our marriage preparation weekend in Park Ridge, IL, at St. Paul of the Cross Catholic Church on May 10, 2002, in a meeting room next to the church. Mark and his family moved to Park Ridge in 1982 when he was fifteen years old. When I relocated to Chicago in 2000 for my job, I lived in downtown Chicago. As we prepared for our life together, we decided it made sense to live in Park Ridge. We rented a condominium in this quaint little town, which is about fifteen miles outside of Chicago. We enjoyed going to Mass at St. Paul of the Cross. Mark's mom was a lector and a Eucharistic minister at the church. It is a beautiful and traditional setting, and I always felt a sense of reverence there.

This weekend allowed Mark and I to share our hopes, thoughts, and inner feelings about becoming man and wife.

Simply put, we wanted to share our love with one another. We wanted to have a family and live our version of happily ever after. Each of us wanted to be the best we could for ourselves and each other. Family values were important to each of us. Integrity was important.

The weekend allowed us to approach those same things in a more "formalized" manner. Because Catholic marriage is a sacrament, the Catholic Church wants couples to be well prepared. The wedding lasts a day and marriage lasts a lifetime. Topics included understanding our own history, communication, money matters, sexual intimacy, love, faith, and creating a marriage based on putting our faith in God's hands. These are "must-have" conversations the Church believes couples must have prior to marriage in the Church.

For two people who found each other on an internet dating website, met in July of 2001, and got engaged the next month, we were so very compatible!

One of our exercises was to write a letter to one another. As I looked back on our history together, I was struck by our exact same greeting to each other.

> My Love,
>
> I can never express in words how much your love has meant to me. I never thought I could find a woman like you who could love me as much as you do. We laugh together and hold each other at night. We have the same beliefs and come from loving families. I can't wait to start a family with you and grow old together. Every day with you brings me more and more happiness. I only hope that I will never let you down, I would die before I would ever let that happen. I can't wait to be your husband.
>
> I love you,
> Mark

My Love,

I have waited all my life to find you—I cannot believe my wishes have come true. You are the person I was meant to spend forever with. Your love is so crystal clear to me—from the moment I made the decision to love you and only you! I know we are a great team—I truly am lucky that God picked you for me. If I were to assemble everything in a man that I was searching for, the final product would be you. You possess every quality that I have ever wanted. What a lucky woman I am! Thank you for loving me and for always making me feel beautiful.

I love you!
Melanie

When planning a wedding, the bride-to-be and groom-to-be are focused on the joyfulness of the pending union; the frenzy and fun of selecting the bridal party, the wedding venue, the photographer, the flowers, the menu, and all of the details to make the day special and memorable.

None of us go into a marriage thinking that illness could take over and end a union sooner than either would have expected . . . or wanted.

I grew up in a suburb just on the outskirts of New Orleans, Louisiana, which is rich in culture and there's always a reason to celebrate!! Think Mardi Gras, festivals, jazz, blues, incredible architecture, and a culture deeply rooted in family (blood relatives, friends, the stranger you pass by on the street). We chose to tie the knot in my hometown of New Orleans on October 5, 2002. Mark knew my love of New Orleans and that my family and friends were all there, so a New Orleans wedding was perfect for us.

The weekend before our wedding, we became aware of a hurricane in the Caribbean and knew we needed to keep an eye on its path. We contacted our Pre-Cana leader and made a contingency plan to have him marry us in Park Ridge in the event we were unable to have our wedding in New Orleans. We were stressed because Mother Nature is unpredictable. Hurricane Lili was threatening to hit the Gulf Coast of Louisiana.

By October 2, it became a major hurricane and was about 365 miles southeast of New Orleans. By this point Mark, his family, and I were in New Orleans. Needless to say, my future in-laws were a wreck. Fortunately, my family was able to reassure and prepare evacuation plans if necessary. Mark's brother and his soon-to-be wife arrived in New Orleans on one of the last flights in, and several guests were unable to travel. Lili made landfall on the morning of October 3, west of New Orleans, as a category one hurricane, with wind gusts reaching 120 miles per hour.

We were married at St. Francis Xavier, a small, quaint church in Old Metairie, Louisiana. Our ceremony was officiated by the bishop, the monsignor, and my sweet (now deceased) uncle Rodney, a deacon. The church was filled with beautiful blue curiosa roses and a candlelit aisle. A dear friend (now a priest) played the music for our special day.

I vividly recall the subtle moments of our wedding, just like it was yesterday. I remember pulling up to the church in a black stretch limousine accompanied by my dear father. We made our way out of the limousine and quickly entered the church. I could not wait to walk up that aisle! I could not wait to see my husband-to-be. The photographer was snapping pictures, as I was hidden away in the church entryway. There was joy and excitement in the air. And finally, Dad and I locked arms and walked up the aisle, with Canon in D beautifully played. Dad gave his little girl away to begin life with this man who made her so happy.

How blessed I was to have my sweet Daddy with me on

the day I always imagined. Dad was always my rock and was relinquishing his position to my soon-to-be husband.

This was the day I dreamed of! On October 5, 2002, at 6:30 p.m., I was on the brink of fulfilling my girlhood dream. The stuff that dreams are made of rarely include the stark reality of the adverse.

We stated our love for one another and shared the traditional wedding vows:

> I, Melanie, take you, Mark, to be my husband, to have and to hold from this day forward, for better, for worse, for richer, for poorer, in sickness and in health, until death do us part.
>
> I, Mark, take you, Melanie, to be my wife, to have and to hold from this day forward, for better, for worse, for richer, for poorer, in sickness and in health, until death do us part.

To have and to hold.
For better.
For worse.
For richer.
For poorer.
In sickness.
In health.
Until death do us part.

Wedding vows are meant to express the intent and the promise of a couple's path as they begin a new life together as one. The vows are the foundation of a marriage and spoken with the intent of the couple to be there for one another despite the circumstances of life.

During the blessing of our marriage, my uncle said, "May Melanie and Mark be blessed with children." He said this a half dozen times. It was very special, as he knew we wanted to immediately begin our family.

Throughout my life, I was blessed to have my parents, grandparents, and many family members who taught me the power of prayer. My Grandmother, affectionately referred to as Tippy, and my mom regularly prayed novenas. A novena is an ancient devotion that consists of consecutive days or weeks of prayer, and it's typically for special intentions. One of the saints I have a devotion to is St. Joseph. At the very bottom of the prayer card, it says, "Pray for nine mornings for anything you may desire. It has never been known to fail, so be sure you really want what you ask for." I said this novena to St. Joseph, and prayed for him to intercede in helping me to find my life partner.

Prayer to St. Joseph

Oh St. Joseph whose protection is so great, so strong, so prompt before the Throne of God. I place in you all my interests and desires.

Oh St. Joseph assist me by your powerful intercession and obtain for me from your Divine Son all spiritual blessings through Jesus Christ, Our Lord; so that having engaged here below your heavenly power I may offer my Thanksgiving and Homage to the most Loving of Fathers.

Oh St. Joseph, I never weary contemplating you and Jesus asleep in your arms. I dare not approach while He reposes near your heart.

Press Him in my name and kiss His fine head for me, and ask Him to return the Kiss when I draw my dying breath. St. Joseph, patron of departing souls, pray for us. Amen.

www.ourcatholicprayers.com

Through my faith and devotion, my path entered Mark's world. I chose Mark to become my husband, and he chose me. Our plan was to grow old together, but God had a different plan in place for both of us. If I would have known then what I know now, I would love this man all over again.

Marriage is a commitment. Wedding vows are an expression of that commitment. Commitment is a lost art today, and although it was not easy, Mark and I maintained our commitment to each other until he was no longer on this Earth.

Despite the unknown future, the fear, the frustration, and knowing that at some point the end would come, we still loved one another and held on to that commitment we made at a small, quaint church in Old Metairie, Louisiana . . .

To have and to hold from this day forward, for better, for worse, for richer, for poorer, in sickness and in health, until death do us part.

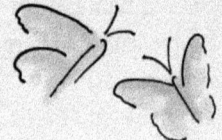

Beloved, do not be surprised at the fiery ordeal among you, which comes upon you for your testing, as though some strange thing were happening to you; but to the degree that you share the sufferings of Christ, keep on rejoicing, so that also at the revelation of His glory you may rejoice with exultation.

1 Pet. 4:12–13 (New American Standard Bible)

The First Hurdle

Our married life was fairly ordinary; we enjoyed the simple things in life, spending time with family, enjoying the variety of things available to do in the Chicago area. Mark was busy with his banking career, and I was working in my human resources role at a restaurant company.

We lived near Mark's parents in the sweet town of Park Ridge, Illinois, and were ready to immediately start a family. Looking back, this was a big topic for us in our "getting to know you days" on the telephone while I was in Washington, DC, that fateful week we fell in love. Both of us wanted to have children.

At thirty-seven years old, we knew we needed to get busy quickly as the biological clock was ticking. I began tracking ovulation timing and scheduling baby-making moments with Mark. After about six months of trying to conceive without success, I consulted with my OB-GYN. He began doing routine testing to check the viability for me to have a child. During my last fertility test, my doctor did what is known as a postcoital test, which indicated Mark's sperm weren't showing up.

At this point, we learned I was fertile, and it was possible that Mark was not. Mark agreed to undergo fertility testing. His doctor performed a few tests, including a testicular biopsy, which was done at a local hospital. My sweet mother-in-law accompanied us to the hospital when he had the procedure. All three of us drove to the hospital together without a lot of conversation; we were apprehensive. This was it! The final straw to determine if we would be able to be parents to a sweet baby girl or boy—whose names were already selected during our getting-to-know-you days. Mark really wanted our baby girl named after his mom's sister, Josephine, who passed away at an early age, and he wanted to call her Josie.

My mother-in-law and I were in the waiting room patiently waiting for the doctor to let us know how things were going. After what seemed like an eternity, the doctor greeted us; Mark was in the recovery room. The doctor shared the cold, hard facts that my husband would never be able to father a child. Our child. He explained that Mark had a condition known as Sertoli-cell-only; simply put, it is the absence of the production of sperm. After the doctor left us, I had a major epiphany. I recall thinking about the people you encounter in life who are bitter and unhappy. It struck me that it was likely that these cranky and unhappy people had a defining moment in life that caused them to be like this. Sitting in the waiting area in the hospital in Park Ridge, Illinois, I was amid a moment that would define me.

With my mother-in-law sitting alongside me, I thought out loud that I had a choice with how I received this news. I could either accept it and figure out how to work through this with my husband, or I could be angry, sad, and bitter for life.

I remember going into the recovery room, and Mark asked me the outcome—the doctor had spoken to him, but he was still woozy from the anesthesia. I told him of the news and quickly followed up by reassuring him that we would be okay. After several hours, we left the hospital and headed home with our crushed dreams.

All I ever wanted from an early age was to be a mother. Mark wanted to be a father. What kind of cruel joke was God playing on us? Both of us struggled with our new reality.

Mark felt like he was letting me down; he felt responsible for our situation, and I couldn't help but be depressed. From my early lessons in religious studies, I deeply knew that my God is not, nor was not, one who punished. The stark reality of not being able to conceive a child hit me to my very core. My faith was shaken.

Life continued for us, and we tried to focus on the positive things in life. We were both internally struggling in our own way. My nature is to solve problems. I embarked on research to adopt, and entertained the idea of a sperm donor so that we could achieve our desire to have a family. Mark half-heartedly listened to my research findings as I eagerly shared options to adopt through Catholic Charities USA or other avenues.

We started the search to purchase our first home. We spent a few weekends with our Realtor touring homes without luck. One day, I received a call from the Realtor to drop everything and check out a home she had recently toured. My mother-in-law and I took a ride to check it out. As soon as I walked in, it was love at first sight: a three-story townhome in a small community that had our name on it. It was everything we were looking for—spacious, well-appointed, and conveniently close to the local tollways. That evening, Mark checked it out with me, and we sealed the deal! We purchased our first home in April of 2004 in Roselle, IL.

I remember move-in day; the movers took forever to get everything from our condo to our new home. Moving for me was old hat, and I am the type that wants to unpack and get settled as quickly as possible. The morning after we moved in, Mark awakened with flu-like symptoms. He stayed in bed all day, and I was determined to get our home set up. And, of course, I did, because that is what I do. My general nature is to simply make it happen. I was undeterred by Mark's inability to help, and I was determined to set up our home. The following day, my sweetheart was much better and was astounded and grateful that everything was in its place.

I was still struggling with the reality of our infertility, and continued researching options. Mark was sad, shattered, but more agreeable to acceptance. Mark's general nature was to accept what was in front of him. He was more of a peaceful person and inclined to accept versus me who always sought a solution or remedy. My parents came up for a visit to check out our new home and spend time with us. My parents and I went to a seminar on international adoption. Mark was unable to join us as he had to work. I excitedly shared everything I learned at the seminar, and Mark said his usual, "I'll think about it."

After months of my research and his pondering over my findings, I was at my wits' end. I was frustrated that I was doing all of this research to solve our situation and to be able to become parents. I wasn't listening to Mark's thoughts, and he wasn't listening to mine. We were both sad, never angry—just sad and disappointed. On a Sunday afternoon, we headed out to the driving range to hit some golf balls. As we wrapped up, we got in the car and I broke down sobbing uncontrollably. It came from out of nowhere, and Mark was trying his best to calm me. Finally, I said through my sadness and tears that I was struggling with our circumstances and that it didn't seem he had interest in exploring other options.

He admitted to me that he was very reluctant to adopt, and he was not interested in going the sperm donor route. He was fearful of the unknown with adopting a child and the potential of dealing with a host of psychological issues or even fetal alcohol syndrome. I was angry and dejected that he was making this decision and not considering the impact on me.

At this point, he took my face in his hands and looked me in the eyes. He said he was so very sorry that we were unable to have children together. He asked me if having children was so important to me, and said he understood if I needed to leave him to move on to pursue this. I sobbed. He sobbed. I could not hold him responsible; it was not his choice to be infertile. As disappointed as I was, I was not going to leave Mark. This was a "better or worse" vow marker. I chose to maintain my commitment to love and honor.

Our desire to have children was not in the plan. God knew what was best for us, but we were unable to see that at the time. My faith was shaken at this point of my life. Looking back on our wedding day, I recall my uncle's marriage blessing. He must have said "bless this couple with children" a half dozen times.

WHY?

WHY?

WHY, OH WHY?

That was all I could say to God at this time in my life. I lost my way for a bit; I stopped leaning on God. It was difficult to go to Mass. On the Sundays that I did attend, I felt sad, empty, and disconnected. I didn't feel the peace I typically felt as soon as I walked into Church. I skipped going to Mass altogether sometimes because I felt abandoned.

I made an appointment with the pastor of St. Paul of the Cross to talk about my thoughts and feelings. I shared my story and that I struggled with understanding why this was the path that was created for us. He reminded me that it is okay to ask why, it is okay to be upset with God, but to not stay in that place. He encouraged me to share my feelings when necessary and not to bottle them up. I really do not recall the entire conversation but that it was an important step for me to take. It helped me to sort through my sadness and helped me to start crawling back to my relationship with God.

Looking back, I was struggling with acceptance of the impact of this on my Sweetheart. It was hard to accept that someone like Mark was dealt this crap hand. It broke my heart to see him wrestling with his own sadness, which it was not in his control to fix. It broke my heart to see him feeling like he was unable to make his girl happy and fulfill a dream we both had.

Mark's brother married around the same time we did. As we were dealing with our reality, we got the news that they were expecting their first child together. As happy as I was for them, I was devastated for us. It was an emotionally charged time for me. It all felt so unfair.

I recalled the sentiment I had when I was in the hospital waiting room when I learned of Mark's infertility. I could continue feeling sad, hurt, and angry, but that was not who I wanted to be. I did not want to be a person who allowed a moment in time to define me. I deserved better, and my husband deserved better.

We decided to accept that our family was just he and I, and that was enough. We were blessed with a nephew, and we were asked to be his godparents. Now that was a blessing for us! Mark loved that baby boy so much. They had a sweet bond up until the time of Mark's death. Additionally, I am godmother to my cousin's daughter, so we had our girl and our boy godchildren. We accepted that we would never have our own children but were grateful we had children in our lives to love and spoil.

This marked our first hurdle as a married couple. Our wedding vows came in to play here. For better or for worse. When we do not get what we want in a relationship, it can be easy to walk away. However, we chose to honor our commitment to being together during the good and bad times. We chose to stay together. I chose to stay in this marriage because Mark was more important to me than not having his child. Looking back to our wedding day, our ceremony and the blessings bestowed upon us, it was difficult to logically wrap my head around not being able to have a child with Mark.

In those dark days of wrestling with our reality, God knew what He was doing. Faith is believing that what He has in store for you is in your best interest even when it does not feel like it. My faith was restored as I focused on living in the present, being grateful for Mark and our marriage, and enjoying each day as a gift.

We accepted the plan that was created for us, and, looking back, it made sense.

And the peace of God, which surpasses all understanding, will guard your hearts and your minds in Christ Jesus.

Phil. 4:7
(English Standard Version)

Something Is Wrong

AS WE SETTLED INTO OUR life as a couple without children, our objective was simply to enjoy what we had together. We enjoyed dining out, traveling, and twilight golf on Friday evenings. Like most families, we had our share of ups and downs; job stress, loss, death of loved ones, and the challenges that life sends our way. Overall, we were good—we were happy, we took care of each other, and we remained each other's best friend.

In July of 2007, Mark had a cough that continued to linger throughout the remainder of the year. Also, he was dealing with severe foot pain that was initially diagnosed as gout, which is a form of inflammatory arthritis that develops in some people who have high levels of uric acid in the blood. The acid can form needle-like crystals in a joint and cause sudden, severe episodes of pain, tenderness, redness, warmth, and swelling. His doctor put him on medication to help alleviate the pain and swelling, but Mark never really felt relief.

Into spring of 2008, the chronic cough continued, the pain in his feet worsened, and now he didn't have much feeling in his feet. He began seeing a neurologist who ordered a slew of bloodwork and other tests to determine the root cause. There was one test result that came back as abnormal, but the doctors really were not concerned. He was diagnosed with peripheral neuropathy, which is damage to the nerves and causes weakness, numbness, and pain, usually in the hands and feet. At this point, only Mark's feet were affected. His doctor prescribed several medications that he did not respond well to. I witnessed my free-spirited husband turn zombie-like, unable to get out of bed due to the side effects of the drugs. We quickly decided this was not the best course of action for him.

The cough continued, and Mark continued to plug along, trying to work and live life despite the pain he was experiencing. He actually broke his ankle but did not even know it due to the lack of feeling in his ankle/feet. He was given a cast and again plugged along.

On November 11, 2008, I arrived home from work after spending the day in Wisconsin. When I entered our home, I vividly recall Mark sitting on the sofa and happily welcoming me home. It was a typical evening. We stayed downstairs for a bit, catching up and watching TV. After we went upstairs to bed, Mark began shaking and vomiting. This all came out of the blue as he didn't exhibit signs of distress or sickness until this moment. I called 911, and the paramedics quickly came and took Mark to the hospital.

Mark was admitted to the hospital for observation and testing. This was our very first time at Alexian Brothers Hospital, as we had recently moved to the area. Mark's previous doctors were not part of this hospital network, so Mark was assigned a hospitalist, a dedicated doctor who works exclusively in a hospital. I was incredibly worried about Mark, since he had started with symptoms in mid-2007 and had continued to suffer rather that improve. I explained in great detail to this doctor everything that Mark went through, along with noting his weight loss and change in appetite. I am forever grateful to Dr. Andrews for listening to me—he hung on to my every word and called in every specialist necessary to get to the bottom of what was going on with my Love.

Those seven days in the hospital were the first of many, and we had no idea what was ahead. At one point, Mark was running an extremely high temperature and was delusional. I was so concerned with what was going on that I spoke to the nurse who called the doctor. They ordered a brain scan due to his change in mental status. I stayed by his side, sponging him with cold water to help get his fever down. As I look back, this was my bootcamp training to begin patient advocacy for Mark. I asked the doctors and nurses every question I had, took copious notes, requested his records, and relied on family and friends who were medical professionals to help guide me. This is the point in our journey where I learned that every patient MUST have an advocate. There are too many moving pieces, and I was the one with a vested interest in my Sweetheart.

Mark had pneumonia and a blood infection. His doctor ordered scans and bloodwork to help diagnose Mark's condition. The tests came back showing he had two different illnesses: a form of cancer called lymphoma; and amyloidosis, which is a rare and serious protein deposition disease . . . it is an abnormal protein that is produced in bone marrow and can be deposited in tissues or organs.

At first, based on the test results, his doctors were leaning toward Mark having mantle cell lymphoma, which is an aggressive and rare form of lymphoma. We were SO SCARED. I remember crying out to my father-in-law that I could not handle this. I laid next to Mark in his hospital bed, and we both just held one another. As we feared the worst, he sweetly asked me what I was going to do, and he insisted I move back to my family in New Orleans. He told me to be happy. I couldn't bear to think about life without him. I clung to my faith and hope that he would be cured and healed.

Maybe he was. For a short time.

The doctors wanted to discharge Mark to Northwestern

Memorial Hospital or University of Chicago Medical Center so he could get elevated care. My hard-headed sweet man refused. He wanted to go home to get some things situated and ensure our finances and such were in order. Mark made certain that we were living our lives as fiscally responsible adults, and he wanted to make sure all our affairs were in order. The doctors agreed to this, and he was discharged home rather than to another hospital.

Mark insisted upon having a "normal" Thanksgiving and did not want to deal with doctor's appointments until afterward. He met with the wonderful Dr. Jane Winter at Northwestern, and she reviewed his medical records and ordered a bone marrow biopsy for the following week and additional bloodwork. After he went through all of the testing, they were able to determine the amyloid was regulated to his lymph nodes (a really good thing in this situation), and the lymphoma wound up being a low-grade version instead of the aggressive form they initially thought he had. FAITH? PRAYERS? Yes!

He began chemotherapy on the day before New Year's Eve with sweet Nurse Judy, and because his blood pressure was so low, they needed to administer the rest of the dose on New Year's Eve. On New Year's Day 2009, I had to take my Sweetheart to the ER as he had severe nausea and vomiting.

He went through eight rounds of chemotherapy like a champ. I worked from the cancer center while the drugs to help him were pumped into his body. Those powerful drugs that caused his body to fold were meant to help him, but it was hard to witness the effects of the chemo on the man I loved. He really was a champ; Mark never complained. He took the chemo, went home, got sick, dealt with it, and continued to work for as long as he could.

At this point, Mark was diagnosed with Charcot foot, which is a weakening of the bones in the foot due to nerve damage, and his right foot was casted. All in all, he had three surgeries on his ankles and required braces for stabilization.

We scheduled a trip to the Mayo clinic in Rochester, Minnesota, with a leading specialist in amyloidosis. By this point, I had earned my MD via the internet on anything and everything related to Mark's illness. I spent many sleepless nights in front of the computer learning everything I possibly could to be my husband's advocate. I joined online groups to help expose me to other people in the same boat. I became a student so that I could be the voice of my husband.

Mark's parents accompanied us on this trip to help support us. Mayo Clinic is an amazing campus, and they took excellent care of Mark. On day one, we registered and Mark gave about a gallon of blood for all of the necessary tests (not really but it seemed like it!). We arrived at the appointment with Dr. Morrie Gertz, and I handed over all of Mark's previous bloodwork results, scans, and many other medical records. It was a stack that was probably ten inches. I also created a medical timeline for Mark to show bullet points of the history since the cough began in July of 2007.

All four of us entered Dr. Gertz's office. He evaluated Mark and looked at me and thanked me for providing him with ALL of the medical records but was most grateful for the timeline. He then asked if I was a nurse. I said I was not but that I had taken the time to learn everything I could to help Mark along the way.

After undergoing extensive testing, the conclusion was that Mark did indeed have a low-grade form of lymphoma and the amyloid was something to continue to keep an eye on. He also had a nerve biopsy while at Mayo to see if the amyloid protein was in his nerves. Thankfully, it was not.

From 2007 until the end of Mark's life, he was hospitalized many times. There were good and bad doctors, and my best advice to anyone standing along the side of their loved one is to learn all that you can about their illness, ask questions, and if you are uncomfortable with the course of treatment, seek another opinion. The irony of medicine is that the term "practicing" medicine is 100 percent accurate. Doctors are not God nor are they superheroes. They are human beings, and mistakes can be made by medical professionals.

Ask those questions, challenge the suggested course of treatment. Ask the doctor, "If this was your brother/sister/spouse/mother/father/child, what would you do?"

If you can believe, all things are possible to him who believes.

Mark 9:23
(New King James Version)

The Move

Throughout 2014 and 2015 Mark had a few hospitalizations, and it was getting increasingly difficult for him to navigate the stairs in our home. Our beautiful townhome was where we spent most of our married life together; we loved it—the area and our dear neighbors, Ron and Debbie. Ron was also battling some health concerns, so he and Mark leaned on each other during those days when both wives were working. As caretakers, Debbie and I were a support for one another, too.

We began house-hunting for a ranch style home in St. Charles, IL, which is only about eighteen miles farther west. We chose St. Charles because it is a beautiful country setting, and most importantly it was where his parents lived. They continued to play a supportive role for both of us, and to make it easier on all of us made the most sense.

At the end of July, after things had settled from the most recent hospitalization, Mark's mom found a cute corner lot ranch on an acre and a quarter. The home was on Cloverfield Circle and felt like country living, with the convenience of the city life only a few short miles away. The grounds were a park-like setting with beautiful gardens filled with roses, hydrangeas, wildflowers, and several varieties of hostas. It was perfect for us. I left the sellers a note to let them know how we felt about their home:

Dearest Homeowner —

My husband and I are smitten with your home.

We can tell you have lovingly taken excellent care over the years.

We hope to begin our next chapter here and will love this home as much as you have.

Sincerely,
Melanie and Mark

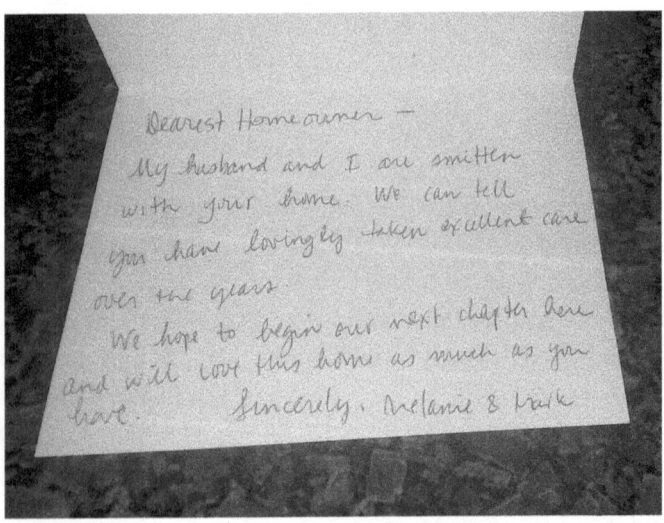

We began envisioning our life in this new setting and getting excited about our next chapter together. Unfortunately, we were unable to sell our home and our offer fell through. Needless to say, we were disappointed. We continued looking at options online. My mother-in-law and I would visit open houses and ride around scouting out the perfect home. Eventually, summer turned to fall, and we decided to take our home off the market with the plan to try to sell again in the spring.

In early 2016, Mark was contacted by a Realtor who pretty much guaranteed he could quickly sell our home. We discussed a game plan, looked online, and much to our surprise, "our" ranch on Cloverfield Circle was *still* available for sale! What are the odds that this would happen?! We put our home on the market, and everything worked out this time for us.

Many Catholics and people of other religious beliefs believe burying a statue of St. Joseph can help with the quick sale of a home. St. Joseph sacrificed his home for his family and made a new home no matter where they went. It is for this reason that people pray to St. Joseph to help them find a new home or help with the sale of their existing one.

We planned a trip to Disney World in March and were looking forward to a nice getaway. Mark's health was okay at this point and only required a motorized scooter to get around. We stayed at the lovely Ritz Carlton in Orlando. Our days at the parks were rather short; Mark's stamina and comfort dictated the length of our day. We enjoyed so many things and created wonderful memories. When we got back to the hotel property, Mark spent most of his time resting. A few evenings, he told me to go to the restaurant to have dinner while he stayed in the room, so I would go downstairs and dine solo and he would order room service. I was feeling particularly sorry for myself on these nights as I watched couples and families dine together. The empty seat across from me was a glimmer of what was to come.

In the middle of our final night, Mark was in an incredible amount of pain in his lower back. I called the hotel front desk very early the next morning to explore our options and decided to call a medical concierge—who knew such a thing existed. A board-certified physician was deployed to our hotel room. She examined Mark and took vitals, a physical exam, and a urine test. His urine specimen was bright red, most likely indicating kidney issues. Our flight home was scheduled midday. Mark was transported to the Orlando hospital via ambulance, and I rode shotgun in dismay that *this* was happening. He was examined by the doctor and diagnosed with kidney stones. We were strongly advised NOT to fly home, which was completely impossible. I was able to change our flight to a late evening flight, and by the sheer grace of God we got home.

The next morning Mark asked me to call the paramedics because he was in too much pain to make it to the hospital in our car. The emergency room doctor informed us that on top of the kidney stones, Mark had pneumonia, had gone into septic shock, and had incredibly low oxygen levels. He was hospitalized for two weeks this round. The doctor was still keeping an eye on the swollen lymph nodes that continued to grow since the July 2015 hospitalization. His oncologist wanted to possibly do some chemotherapy, but Mark was opposed. After his first week of being in the hospital, I put in a request for a leave of absence so that I could support Mark rather than balancing both work and my sweet husband. He was discharged home with IV antibiotics. I had to be trained on how to administer the meds via his port and maintained meticulous records to ensure I was on top of everything.

For the balance of March and the first few weeks of April, Mark regained his strength. I returned to work full time after taking a few weeks off. It was apparent that his body was beginning to weaken and his ability to walk long distances and maneuver around was decreasing. We just went with the flow, did what we could, and managed based on Mark's stamina. Prior to this hospitalization, Mark was able to get himself dressed and prepare breakfast or lunch for himself. This was no longer the case, and he became more dependent on me to help him.

The new home that we purchased was closing on Tax Day! We had sold our townhome and were represented by our attorney and closed on our new home. We moved out of our townhome and into our new home in one day. Thankfully, we had the movers pack us, load, and unload all of our belongings. The movers rolled Mark into our new home in his wheelchair on the ramp they had set up. The movers got our furniture set up, placed boxes in the rooms they needed to be in, and set up our beds. It was a long day, but we were happy to be in our new home.

The very next day, I left our new home filled with unpacked boxes and went to a work meeting. I remember pulling out of our driveway early that morning, and neighborhood kids awaiting their school bus waved to me as I drove down the street. I loved the small-town feel!

Those unpacked boxes needed to get unpacked, and Mark really was not able to help me. I returned home from work, and my dear in-laws pitched in to help me. My entire kitchen was set up with all of the cabinets lined with shelf-liners so everything was ready for me to simply unload the boxes. My mother-in-law scrubbed bathtubs, toilets, and whatever else to make sure my workload was minimal. My father-in-law helped me to set up everything we needed from a maintenance standpoint. Since we were now living on a well, that became the new source of water in our home. We needed water softeners and a reverse osmosis system set up so that our drinking water and ice were purified and filtered.

Moving is one of the most stressful things in life, and to add a chronically ill husband to that equation increases the stress factor. However, we *just did it*. We put one foot in front of the other, literally and figuratively, to move forward and just do what we needed to do for us. We really took it all in stride, and I knew God was there walking along side of us to make sure we didn't fold under the stress.

From April until November 13, 2016, we thoroughly enjoyed settling into our new home. The parade of flowers was simply spectacular. We had peonies, lilies, and irises to greet us for our first spring. It was typical to see deer and ducks hanging out. We put out a hummingbird feeder, and much to Mark's delight, a hummingbird immediately appeared! We loved being outdoors and on our deck. At this point, Mark's health was relatively stable. Nevertheless, he couldn't get around easily, used a walker for the most part, and his stamina was low. Though our moments together were easy and always within the confines of what he could handle, we intentionally chose to focus on what we could do together, while I continued to remain protective of his needs.

We enjoyed exploring our new neighborhood and had a few sleepovers with our nephews who lived around the corner. We enjoyed this country living and the peace and tranquility that came along with our new home. Our weekends were spent on the deck relaxing, and we did a lot of grilling—our favorite. We loved to entertain and took every opportunity to celebrate. Mark always loved celebrating his birthday, so we combined his birthday with a housewarming and had family and friends join us for a dinner party in May.

We explored numerous restaurants, enjoyed the local festivals but mostly loved just being together. It was getting a bit more difficult for him to navigate, so we used his transporter wheelchair I purchased. At first, he was reluctant to be in a wheelchair, but he adapted and knew it was best. Of all the things we did, Mark told me that lying in bed next to each other was his favorite time together. I learned this is when he felt most "normal" without the confines of a walker or wheelchair. Normal was his word—he felt free lying in bed.

We loved our new home, and I only had one complaint—the stove wasn't the greatest. I love to cook! Mark knew how much I loved my gas stove and convection oven left behind in our previous home. Leave it to my husband to surprise me with a new gas stove with convection oven for my birthday on August 25. This was my Mark—kind and generous and always wanting to please his girl.

Fall was upon us, and our usual outing to the pumpkin patch involved only me this year. I was happy to maintain our tradition of decorating but saddened that I had to do it all alone. It was becoming increasingly difficult for Mark to get out and around; he simply did not have the energy. We rolled with it. We simply did what we *could* do together and didn't focus on what we *could not* do. A simple drive through the car wash on a Sunday, hanging out on the deck enjoying fresh air, or chilling together was enough.

So do not fear, for I am with you; do not be dismayed, for I am your God. I will strengthen you and help you; I will uphold you with my righteous right hand.

Isa. 41:10 (NIV)

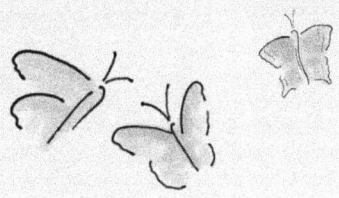

The Beginning of the End

ON NOVEMBER 13, 2016, OUR niece was married at the Herrington Inn in Geneva, IL. Although Geneva is a short distance away from our former home, Mark insisted we make a weekend out of it and spend the night at the hotel. By this point, he required a wheelchair to navigate long distances and simply did not have the energy to use his walker. Early the next morning, Mark awakened me to tell me he felt a burning in his stomach and did not feel well. The pain continued, and I called the paramedics to take him to the hospital. Mark had already established care with a new set of doctors in the area since our move, but this was the first of many trips to the new hospital.

It is difficult to describe how I felt during this first trip to the new hospital, as we had to establish care in a whole new system. Up until now, Mark was a "regular" at Alexian Brothers near our previous home, and the staff knew Mark and his condition, but now he was new and we were new and the doctors were new. Mark was in an extreme amount of pain. In large part, the pain was due to peripheral neuropathy, but it is really hard to know exactly what was going on inside of him. Peripheral neuropathy is the medical term used to describe nerve damage that causes weakness, numbness, and pain. By this point, the pain was in his hands and feet. For Mark, the doctors were never able to uncover the cause of the neuropathy, only that it was idiopathic. He described the pain as a stabbing and burning feeling, which worsened at night or during cold or rainy weather. His pain was constant. Day to day, we managed pain control with meds, but Mark's sweet nature generally remained intact. His pain would increase with environmental factors—if it was cold or rainy, he always experienced a deeper sense of pain.

He was on Vicodin—or shall I say, the evil opioids—to help control his pain on a regular basis. When he asked for pain medication, I swear we were made to feel like he was a drug seeker. It was the oddest feeling to try to explain his condition. Given the length of his illness, it made it seem like all we were looking for was a fix. I completely understand that there is a segment of the population that abuses opioids and there is reference to an opioid epidemic, but that is where I take issue personally. Mark was NOT seeking a fix; he was seeking relief from an unbearable and indescribable pain. As his advocate, I tried to explain and help his cause. The ER doctor gave him a small amount of pain meds and discharged him as his only symptoms were pain and nausea.

The following day, Mark went back to the hospital with the same symptoms and was admitted. His new doctor met with us and elected to give him a fentanyl patch to help with the pain. The new oncologist ordered CAT scans, endoscopy, and several other tests. The next few days were all about keeping him comfortable and running tests to help his new team of doctors get a baseline.

In the early morning hours on November 18, I received a call from the hospital. For those who have been there, a call in the middle of the night from a hospital when your loved one is there can send your heartrate through the roof. The rapid response nurse identified herself and calmly explained what was going on. Mark aspirated his stomach contents and was in ICU where the ICU doctor would be intubating him to place him on a ventilator. I do not even know how

I managed to get myself dressed and drive to the hospital. I know God was carrying me as I kept telling myself, "Just breathe, it will be okay, just breathe, it will be okay." I called Mark's parents to let them know what was going on, and his dad met me at the hospital. I got there so quickly, I was able to see Mark before he was put on the vent. I kept a brave face and was the strength that I knew he needed. After the intubation, the doctor met with my father-in-law and I and explained that Mark was doing okay but that it was a difficult intubation. As diligent an advocate as I was, I didn't have the energy to really understand what this meant ... months later, the impact of this showed up.

I was with Mark when he awakened from the anesthesia and fully realized he had a vent doing his breathing for him. His wrists were restrained—a protocol for intubated patients to ensure they do not remove the tube from their mouth. I vividly recall he was moving each wrist up and down, almost puppet-like, as he tried to figure out why he was restrained. It was hard to watch, but my calm kicked in and I helped soothe him.

I spent long days and nights at the hospital with Mark and recall feeling afraid. I always remained calm and composed while Mark was intubated, as I was the anchor for him during this time. I relied on prayers from loved ones near and far to help keep us bathed in love and strength during this difficult time. During this time, I was working from the hospital and not yet on a leave of absence so that I could be with Mark. The ICU team graciously allowed me to stay with Mark outside of visiting hours. I spent time in the hospital chapel to help keep me calm and plugged into prayer and to have a quiet place to just exhale.

I happened upon the following entry in a journal that was available for visitors to leave thoughts and prayers. Imagine my dismay when I realized this entry was written on our wedding anniversary date. I have no idea who wrote this but took comfort in the words and couldn't help but see this as a foreshadowing of what was to come.

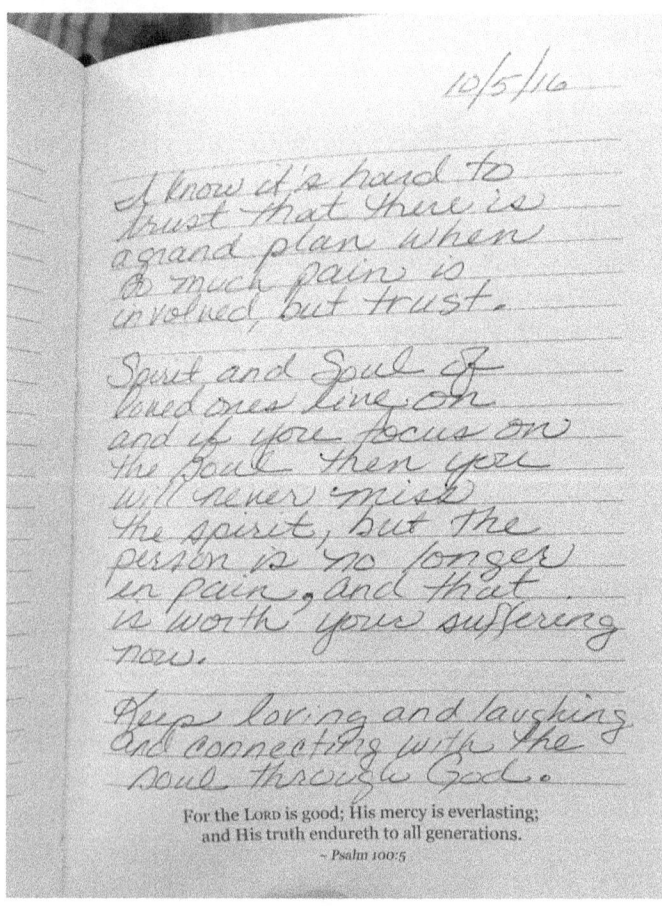

Mark was able to be trusted to have the restraints removed (thank you, Jesus), and we quickly learned how to communicate with the iPad, with him pointing to the letter on the keyboard to make a sentence or word. Gratefully, a few days later, the vent was removed, and he remained in ICU.

When Mark started having difficulty breathing and his oxygen levels became too low, he was required to be intubated again. This round he was on the ventilator for about five days. He spent Thanksgiving in ICU. I recall our plans were to have Thanksgiving in our new home with my family and his ... not in the ICU. My parents carried on with their plans to visit to help support us. We had Thanksgiving cookies that we shared with everyone who was tending to Mark and working on that Thanksgiving Day ... our little way of saying thank you for taking care of us. Even in his sickness, Mark's generosity shined. When anyone came in to tend to him—a housekeeper, respiratory therapist, doctor, or nurse—he would look over to me and raise his chin up to say without words, "Hey babe, give them a cookie."

The day after Thanksgiving, Mark was slated for surgery again. In the midst of this, again the overarching concern was that the amyloid was wreaking havoc on his body, so his medical team wanted to do a biopsy of the abdominal wall (fat pad biopsy) to see if he had systemic amyloidosis. Additionally, Mark had not really had any nutrition for about fourteen days, so his medical team determined it would be best for him to get a jejunostomy tube (J-tube). A J-tube is a soft plastic tube placed through the skin of the abdomen into the midsection of the small intestine. The tube delivers food and medicine until the person is healthy enough to eat by mouth. Little did we know at this point that Mark would never eat again. A few days later, the vent was removed and Mark graduated from the ICU to a CCU step down unit.

On December 7, Mark was discharged to Marianjoy Rehabilitation Hospital. He had to qualify to get into this setting, and the guidelines were set up during intake that he had to show he was involved and willing to participate in the intensive physical, speech, and occupational therapy to help him regain his strength. He settled in well; Mark's nature was to engage with people. He was on a regimented plan and was doing well. A mere FOUR days later, trouble ensued. There was something going on with his feeding tube along with some concerns about his oxygen levels. And off we went in an ambulance back to the hospital. Good God, this poor man just could not get a break. I was sad, angry, and upset that my Love had to deal with yet another hospital admission. My faith waned during this time—I questioned, "WHY?" I wondered why a sweet soul like Mark had to deal with blow after blow after blow. I found it difficult to seek out the Lord, but I went through the motions as I knew I needed to.

In the hospital, Mark was diagnosed with pneumonia (again) and had to undergo surgery to replace his feeding tube. Poor. Sweet. Man. He spent five days there and was discharged back to Marianjoy Rehabilitation Hospital.

It is safe to say, by this point, that Mark's flame was a glimmer. He was tired of the setbacks and of course frustrated by this most recent one. He was not giving his all to the therapy sessions, and this was cause for alarm. I began working from Marianjoy and carving out time to be present when Mark was doing physical, occupational, and speech therapy. I was struggling to balance everything and was barely sleeping to hold everything together. My days were very early as I arrived at Marianjoy by 7:30 and stayed until Mark was finished with dinner. I went home and worked to play catch-up for missed time during the day. I worked with Mark to encourage him, made great connections with the hospital team/staff, and continued to advocate for him. During this time, Mark was introduced to Reiki and aromatherapy, which helped him immensely. In Reiki, the practitioner transfers energy by placing their hands over or on the patient. Practitioners can enable relaxation, reduce pain, speed healing, and reduce other symptoms of illness. Reiki has been around for thousands of years. Mark said he felt calm and less pain after a Reiki session. He became a more active participant in his rehab. When he was doing his PT and walking therapy, I played the theme song from *Rocky* to help keep him motivated . . . he loved it, the *first* time!

Mark's overall strength improved; however, the therapy intended to help strengthen the muscles used when swallowing was not successful. When he swallowed—his saliva or whatever he ate or drank—would go into his lungs. This was attributed to the difficult intubation he had, and could have been from muscle weakness from his overall condition. A test called a swallow study was done, and the results were not encouraging. He was continuing to aspirate when he tried to eat or drink. Our hope was that he would be weaned off the feeding tube, but that was not in the cards.

He was discharged after a total of fifty-nine days away from our home, and we were rejoicing. It was a bittersweet goodbye to the people who helped make an impact on Mark. I had taken a leave of absence and was home with Mark as we acclimated to a new routine with his feeding tube.

The first few days at home were busy with receiving shipments of nutrition for his tube feedings, medical supplies, and installing equipment to help Mark get around with comfort and ease. We were assigned a wonderful team of home health nurses, a speech therapist, and physical and occupational therapists. At this point, Mark was my full-time job. The very best home health care nurse, Maggie, was assigned to Mark. She is a spry Scottish gal with a wonderful sense of humor, a stellar nurse, and a dear friend to this day. The case manager arranged for Mark to get Reiki, and he found so much comfort when Amy came to our home.

My dear cousin, Jenn, flew to Chicago from New Orleans to help lend support to me. She is a nurse practitioner, and having her around to help set up med charts, organize medical supplies, and lend support as we adapted to our new norm was tremendous. I cried like a baby when she left, as I was afraid of the road ahead. Assuming the responsibility to take caretaking to the next level was overwhelming. I returned to work from my leave of absence and began the life of balancing a full-time job along with taking care of Mark.

I leaned into my faith to help guide me and provide me the necessary strength to take great care of my beloved. I never wanted Mark to feel like a burden—ever. Of course, there were times when the feeding tube dislodged and he didn't realize the nutritional liquid spilled all over the chair, floor, and him. He would call out, "Baby, I need you." I would rush in to see what was up and would gently tell him it was okay. I would clean up things, change his clothes, and all would be well.

The gift Mark gave me before he was ever ill was the gift of perspective. His nature was so easygoing, and he really did not sweat the small stuff. If either of us dropped, spilled, or genuinely screwed up, his words were always, "It's okay." His approach was to clean up the spill, fix the screw-up, and NOT freak out. This lesson he taught me early on in our marriage served me well during his illness.

Often, we had doctor's appointments, swallow studies, scans, and blood tests to continue to monitor Mark's health. Mark's dad always accompanied us to the appointments to lend a hand and support us. On days when I worked in the office or traveled out of town for work, my father-in-law assumed the role of caretaker. There were a few times when I was on the road for work where Mark was rushed to the ER due to pain or other complications. Somehow, I always had a sixth sense when this happened. Our security system allowed me to monitor our home on my iPhone and could tell if they left the house in the middle of the night—always an indicator of a trip to the hospital. This happened three or four times. I always hopped the next flight home as that is where I needed to be.

From March through September, Mark had several hospitalizations, paralyzed vocal cords, discussions of possibly doing a tracheostomy, and hospice was suggested in May, but he wasn't ready for this yet.

In mid-September on a Saturday morning, I awakened early to give Mark his meds, start his feeding tube, and empty his catheter. He wanted to rest in bed a little while longer, and I was more than happy to take advantage of the down time. I was lying in bed next to him reading, and I tuned into his breathing. It seemed he was in a deep sleep but was struggling a bit to breathe. Suddenly, he stopped breathing! I jumped onto my feet and was screaming his name at the top of my lungs. I grabbed the phone and called 911. At the same time, Mark sat up in bed, his eyes rolled in the back of his head, and he took in a huge gasp—it was as if he had been under water and was finally coming up for air. He asked what I was doing as I was standing over him with phone in hand, speaking to the dispatcher. I explained I called 911. He insisted I hang up the phone. Of course, I did not.

The paramedics arrived. By this point, we were on a first-name basis, and they were familiar with Mark's health condition. They checked him out and asked him how he was doing. He told them he was fine. I explained what prompted me to call, and Mark quickly chimed in with, "My wife was sleeping, she was dreaming . . . I am fine." They checked his oxygen levels, and his saturation was in the mid- to high sixties (with mid- to high nineties being the norm). The paramedics wanted to take him to the hospital, and he declined. He said he was fine . . . he wasn't. One of the medics told Mark they would honor his request, but if they received another call, this was not like baseball—he would not get three strikes; they would take him to the hospital.

Life continued to plug along. We had a CT scan scheduled and a few other appointments. On Saturday September 30, the doorbell rang. I opened it and was greeted with a beautiful bouquet of lavender roses from Mark to me as an early anniversary surprise. Mark was always about extending a celebration and wanted me to enjoy the flowers over the weekend. Our fifteenth anniversary was on October 5. A few hours later after what was a typical morning, Mark was having trouble breathing again. His oxygen levels were in the 80s. I made what was my last 911 call from our home on Cloverfield Circle. The paramedics came in checked out Mark and quickly got him on his way to the hospital. I did what I always did during these moments: I quietly told myself to just keep taking deep breaths and that it would be okay. It was a routine I had become accustomed to. I met Mark at the hospital.

His usual group of doctors tended to him. One of them spoke to me and said there really was not much more they could do for Mark. He would continue this cycle of going back and forth to the hospital. He suggested we enroll in hospice to help keep Mark comfortable. The following day, he was in septic shock. His body was literally shutting down. I approached my husband about my conversation with the doctor. I wanted to break this to him myself and begin to gently pave the way. Mark, in his usual fashion, said he had to think about it. The following day, his doctor made rounds and discussed what was going on with his health. His lungs were compromised, and he had very little lung capacity. Mark agreed to talk to the hospice team.

Each day of his hospital stay, a volunteer musician would visit us. We loved hearing her beautiful music as a form of relaxation therapy. She sang, played the guitar, and did guided imagery for Mark. His vital signs would naturally level out as this was a peaceful and calming experience. It was reassuring to see him responding to this form of relaxation and comfort.

As I drove home one evening, I was called to go to our church, St. Patrick. I wanted to connect with Monsignor Knox to discuss Mark's impending end of life. I wanted to personally ask him to visit Mark and give last rites and simply seek solace during this difficult time. Confession was being offered during this time, I assumed, but I had no idea if Monsignor was in the confessional. As I stood in line, I noticed that Monsignor was in the pew. As the lines were growing, I then noticed that he went into the empty confessional to hear confession. By the grace of God, I went into his confessional. I explained to him that I was called to the church as I drove home and wanted to directly speak to him that night.

He listened to my concerns, fears, and my confession. Just before I was leaving, he told me that he was not expected to be at church on this particular evening but was called to be there. Instantly, we both knew that God was paving the way for us to connect on that night.

On Mark's last day in the hospital, I was out in the hallway while a respiratory therapist was preparing Mark to go home with oxygen. I overheard him say to one of the therapists that he was scared. Outside of his room were a few other nurses, and they repeated what he said and fought back tears. By this point, so many of the hospital staff knew Mark due to his lengthy and repeated hospitalizations. I began to cry. I knew my sweetheart was afraid, but he never spoke those words aloud to me. He wanted to protect me from his fear. I think we both wanted to shield one another from our own fears.

I have fought the good fight, I have finished the race, I have kept the faith.

2 Tim. 4:7 (NIV)

Home with Hospice

THE PARAMEDICS ENTERED MARK'S HOSPITAL room to take him home for the final time. I privately cued them that he was going home to prepare to go to Heaven. I had arranged for our landscapers to fill our planters with mums and set up bales of hay with pumpkins and gourds to welcome Mark home. Every fall, we would go to the pumpkin patch to select pumpkins and fall flowers to decorate our home. I wanted Mark to enjoy that experience one last time.

We arrived home, and Mark's dad helped us to get settled. This "last time" of going through this process of settling in at home after a hospital stay was much more difficult. My Love was so weak, and it took more effort and strength for my father-in-law and I. Mark insisted upon sitting in his usual chair to watch TV. The hospice nurse arrived to assess Mark and orient us to his care plan. Everyone left, and it was just the two of us. This was definitely the beginning of the end of Mark's life, and neither of us had to say a word about our sadness and fear of what was to come. It was surreal for me, but it was important for me to be strong for Mark. When it was time to get ready for bed, our usual routine of me helping Mark slide over from the chair to the wheelchair was impossible. He no longer had the energy to help support himself, and he felt like dead weight. I had to call my father-in-law to come over and help me. We almost dropped my Sweetheart but managed to get him in the wheelchair and into the bedroom and ultimately in our bed.

The next day I arranged for a hospital bed to be brought in so that Mark would be more comfortable. The bed was set up in the living area and would give him the beautiful view of our deck and backyard. He absolutely did not want to go into the hospital bed, and he said he was more comfortable in our bed ... so that is where he stayed. It was important for me to honor that request; he had to have some control in what was happening to him and around him.

Throughout Mark's illness, I dove in and learned everything I could to be his advocate, to be able to ask good questions and ensure he was getting the best possible care. Logically, I knew this time would come, that Mark would die, but I never allowed myself to think through what Mark's death meant. With the same level of curiosity and care, I researched how to help my husband have a peaceful setting while he transitioned to Heaven. I received a booklet from my soon-to-be sister-in-law to help prepare me for this journey. As I reflect, my pursuit of a peaceful death for my Love was just as much for me as for him. This act of love allowed *me* to prepare mentally, emotionally, and spiritually for what was happening in our home. This was our final time as husband and wife, physically.

Journal entry on 10/4/17:

> **Discharged home with hospice**
>
> **Is comfortable**
>
> **I'm so sad and will miss Mark so but want him to be at peace and comfortable.**
>
> **He loved his music therapy with guided imagery at the hospital.**

> His happy place at home was the deck—being outdoors—we loved to hang out on the deck and enjoy the fresh air.
>
> It is difficult to keep his wish of no hospital bed as he is too hard to transfer.
>
> Had a restful evening; I wanted to talk and say goodbye.
>
> I need to know that I loved enough.

The following day we awakened together in our bed on our fifteenth wedding anniversary. Our last time to say those words to each other on Earth. However, I am so grateful to have loved Mark and been loved by him. We had a marriage that had challenges due to living with an illness that would eventually consume us. We stuck with it, the good times and the hard times. We really did live those vows faithfully. *That* is a blessing.

The nurse visited a few times during the day, along with Mark's brother and his parents. I played relaxing and soothing music for him, and I diffused lavender and frankincense for his aromatherapy. Generally, the lighting was soft and the environment was calm. When music wasn't playing, I played sounds of nature and other white-noise sounds for him to relax to. And, of course, my TV boy had to have his Syfy channel on at night, and, of course, I teased him about watching *Star Trek*. At some point, it struck me; if you just listen to the actors on that show, their voices are incredibly soothing—especially Spock's! During Mark's last days, he was quiet. He would respond when I spoke to him but was quiet and just wanted to be comfortable in our bed.

I put some of our favorite pictures on the dresser in full view for him to look at. Periodically, I opened the window for fresh air to come into the bedroom. I read aloud some of our love letters we emailed to each other in our early days that seemed so long ago and just yesterday all at the same time.

Our priest came to our home to give Mark the Catholic sacrament of "last rites" and to pray with us. This sacrament is received at the end of one's life and includes confession, holy communion, and the anointing of the sick. Mark's mom joined us, and I couldn't help but reflect that she was with her son for his very first sacrament—baptism—and now she was here for his last. Really, a parent should not have to go through this experience. She was a rock, she held me up, she was a tremendous source of support.

Journal entry on 10/5/17:

> **15-year Wedding Anniversary**
>
> Despite where we are, I'd do it all again.
>
> I'm trying to engage Mark to have things/sayings to hold on to.
>
> I asked him his favorite nickname I gave him, and he said Bubba :)

[*Note:* I only started calling him Bubba the last days of his life; I told him it was his southern nickname.]

> I asked him for another, and he said Backscratch.

[*Note:* Now this was FUNNY! I never called him this, but he ALWAYS wanted his back scratched.]

> My Froggie, I love him!
>
> Mark had Last Rites today from Monsignor Knox
>
> Mark wanted his mom to join; it was so peaceful and Mark was accepting.

> I asked him if he wanted to be buried or cremated—buried.
>
> Asked him if he'd still protect me after he got to Heaven—he will!
>
> Asked him how will I know he is with me—butterfly!
>
> I saw 2–3 butterflies this afternoon, and I know it was a sign.
>
> Learning about death now—life is really a gift—we need to treasure the time we have.
>
> Bless my sweet husband. Keep him in the palm of your hand, Sweet Jesus.
>
> Mother Mary, stay with him.
>
> Help him to be not afraid.
>
> I love you, Froggie—Happy Anniversary . . . *AILYS.*

The night quickly turned to morning, and a new day was in front of us. His nurse came early in the day to check in, and Mark's parents stayed with us. Mark seemed to be in more pain, and his breathing was more labored. He was rarely by himself in our bedroom; we each took turns either sitting next to him or lying down in bed with him. On this particular day, it struck me that I needed to discuss funeral plans with my sweet in-laws. I explained that I would be relocating to New Orleans, and I wanted them to choose his final resting place. I remember the dismayed look on my father-in-law's face in response to my plan to move. This was a detail Mark and I discussed very early on in his illness; he wanted to make sure I was back home with my family if anything were to happen to him.

I arranged for the music therapist volunteer to come to our home; she was the same young lady who played for Mark in the hospital. She lovingly played soothing tunes and sang to us. I felt like I was outside of myself as we both laid in bed listening to this angel sing, with the lavender essential oils dispersing in the air in the middle of the day. I allowed myself to be present every second of the day. Of course, my mind would race, but I wanted to make sure my Love was well cared for and loved so deeply during these final days on Earth.

The nurse bumped his pain medication up and indicated he was declining. My learning about death continued daily—who knew a scale exists to measure the progressive decline of a dying person. *My person.* The scale is called the Palliative Performance Scale (PPS), a validated and reliable tool used to assess a patient's functional performance and to determine progression toward end of life. The nurse also increased his intake of oxygen to help him feel more comfortable. I read through some of our letters and also stumbled upon a letter he wrote to my parents after he first met them, dated Wednesday, July 18, 2001.

> Dear Jim and Marilyn,
>
> First let me thank you for the beautiful card; I also had a great time with you. I can see that Melanie comes from a great family and that you two did a great job raising Melanie. Now I know where your daughter gets her looks and good manners.
>
> Right now Melanie is in Atlanta, and I miss her very much; your daughter is the best thing that ever happened to me, and I want you to know that I love her very much, and I will always take care of her and love her with all my heart. I don't know how I got through life before I met your daughter, but I know that I can't imagine life without her in it.

> I am looking forward to coming to New Orleans and seeing where Melanie grew up and seeing you again also. I can't wait to visit the sights and sample the local food. I've always been intrigued by the Big Easy, and now I will finally get to experience it. Maybe Jim and I can get a round of golf in. I am also anxious to meet Melanie's brother—I would love to introduce myself to as many people as I can when I'm down there. I'm sure Melanie has a lot of friends who would like to meet the man she talks about.
>
> Well, I am not much of a letter writer but wanted to say thank you and thank you again for your daughter. I promise I will always love her and make her happy. I will look forward to seeing you again soon, and thank you for being so kind to me.
>
> Sincerely,
> Mark Trimarco

This! This was the essence of my husband—just a kind man who was grateful for the love we shared.

I crawled in bed with Mark at the end of a long day and scribbled the following notes that night.

> Oh, the days go by too quickly . . . Mark's mother is my hero—she's a pillar of dignity and strength, yet I know she is dying on the inside. I appreciate the love and support from both MIL and FIL . . . tonight when it is just Mark and I is my favorite—just US. I'll miss him so much. We're affectionately bumping foreheads—it reminds me of Rudolph the Red-Nosed Reindeer and his girlfriend Clarice . . . *AILYS*, Mark S. Trimarco.

My parents arrived from New Orleans on Saturday, and I was grateful to have them with me to help support me. They

And I Love You So

were both loving and sweet, and I was grateful they were staying with us. My only journal entry on this day was "This was a rally day." Rallying seems to be a normal part of the dying process, as it provides a burst of energy for the individual to tie up loose ends and come to terms with their death. Oddly, rallying plays an important role in the dying process. Mark seemed to be more alert and seemed better. Mark's godfather and his wife visited Mark. My dad was astounded that Mark was sitting up in bed with his leg stretched out like he was just hanging out. We had some laughs and talked a bit. Mark thanked my parents for being there.

The next day was a Sunday, and it was the polar opposite of the previous day. The gunk in his lungs was not coming up when he tried to cough, and I could feel his chest rattling. Our sweet nephews, Mark's brother, and our sister-in-law visited. Mark didn't really say much during the visit, but the boys kept him entertained with their stories and their animation. He smiled, and you could see he was taking it all in. The younger nephew was adamant about visiting his uncle—it is difficult for children to experience end of life with a loved one. However, this made Mark's day. Before the boys visited, I asked him if he was at peace, and he said he wasn't. After those boys left our bedroom, he told me he was at peace. He adored those boys, and he was grateful for that last visit. My heart was full and broken at the same time.

Throughout the day, I told Mark it was okay to go and that Jesus was waiting for him. He constantly wanted something cold to drink—keep in mind that he was unable to swallow without aspirating, so he would take a sip and swish the cold drink in his mouth and spit it out. A few times he swallowed, but it was never a big sip. This running back and forth from the bedroom to the kitchen continued the entire day. I was exhausted. At one point, in the evening, I said, "Baby, you're killin' me." He softly responded, "Don't worry, baby, it will be over soon." Oh, my heart.

He wanted us to get ready for bed around seven p.m., unusually early but I got us tucked in.

Throughout these last days at home, he constantly had *Star Trek* on the television at night, and he wanted a lamp on so we would not be in the dark. On this particular night, he wanted the television off, lights out, and his oxygen off. As I learned in my research, on a loved one's final days, it is important to let them take the lead, as long as whatever they want isn't harmful. So, I complied with his wishes. He just wanted quiet. I silently cried out to all the angels, saints, and loved ones who have gone before us to help Mark have a peaceful death, an easy transition to Heaven. I asked St. Joseph, patron saint of departing souls, to gently help him to go home. I placed a St. Joseph prayer card in between our pillows.

Around three a.m., I awakened to Mark sitting up in bed clutching the St. Joseph prayer card with his right hand. I sat up with him and gently and lovingly spoke to him. Inwardly, I was astonished as Mark had no feeling in his hands at this point and his hands were contorted due to nerve damage. It was impossible for him to actually pick up this card, and I knew that my prayers were being answered.

Mark was looking around as if he was seeing someone or something. He asked me if I had anything to eat, and then he started moving his hand to his mouth as if he were actually eating something. Mark had not spoken of food, asked for food, or even had food since the previous November. I believe he was getting a glimpse of Heaven and a feast was awaiting him. He also spoke of waiting on a driver. He shared a few other things he was witnessing, and I chose to stop asking questions; I just wanted to silently be with him and help to keep him be unafraid.

After a few hours of this, Mark tried to get out of bed as if he had somewhere he needed to go. He also started picking at the sheets. The hospice nurse told me that a dying person experiences restlessness, and the best way to manage this is to inform her early so that we could administer medication to help keep him safe and calm. The exact cause of why this occurs may be related to the body shutting down, causing waste buildup along with organs failing. I knew this was my cue to call the hospice nurse to come to our home to evaluate Mark. I remember wanting to awaken my parents so that I wasn't experiencing all of this alone, but a voice within told me to go through this with just Mark and me. I did let him know I was going to call the nurse, and he said, "Okay." The very last words he said to me before he was medicated were "Go get my iPad" . . . I retrieved it and gave it to him. He then said, "Give it to my ma." Up until the very end, Mark was thinking of others. His mom's tablet had recently stopped working.

The nurse arrived around six a.m., and we administered medication from the comfort kit, which contains medications for pain, anxiety, nausea, insomnia, and breathing problems. We honed in on the meds for anxiety, pain, and breathing problems. After the first dose of morphine was administered, Mark rested peacefully throughout the day while family members stayed with him and we all had our private moments with him.

The sweet music therapist came over and blessed us with peaceful and beautiful songs that helped with the letting-go process. She sang "Somewhere over the Rainbow," "My Way," and "What a Wonderful World," among several others. What she did not know is that two of those songs were on our wedding CD that we gave to our guests as a gift on our wedding day. We had a modern version of "Somewhere over the Rainbow" and "What a Wonderful World," as that was the song we danced to with our parents at our wedding.

Throughout the evening, Mark was comfortably resting. Around eight p.m., my dad and mom came into our bedroom and told me to take some time to eat dinner. I just didn't want to leave his side. Throughout the day, I would check Mark's oxygen level with a device placed on the finger called a pulse oximeter. I did a check, and there was no reading.

My sweet Mark took his last breath at 8:06 p.m. The moment none of us ever wanted had arrived.

His pain and suffering were over.

My grief journey began.

Let us then with confidence draw near to the throne of grace, that we may receive mercy and find grace to help in time of need.

Heb. 4:16 (ESV)

Saying Goodbye

My sweetheart was ill for so long; nine years in total, with the last few being the most debilitating, yet the reality of life without him physically on Earth was not something I could even consider until I HAD to. And while I, of course, grieved the loss of our ability to do things together or to be intimate for many years, I was never really prepared for the stark reality of waking up each morning to an empty place next to me in the bed.

I slept in our bed alone that night, with the reality that this would be permanent—Mark would never be lying next to me again. Ever. I was exhausted after such an emotionally charged night and quickly fell asleep. I awakened the next morning and felt like I had been punched in the gut. Mark was not there. Even during his final days, Mark and I continued to sleep in our bed together so that I could be nearby should he need anything throughout the night. Each morning when I would awaken to my sleeping husband, I could not help but absorb the peacefulness upon his face. Honestly, there were mornings I would envision him in a casket with the same peaceful look on his sweet face. Morbid, I know. However, I knew my man and I were not destined to grow old together. While he was fast asleep, he was missing one key element in his life—PAIN. Our usual routine of me getting his morning meds, cleaning him up, and helping him into the living room was never going to happen again. I knew what was ahead of me—a visit to the funeral home. I was going through all of the motions to prepare for Mark's visitation and burial, but I was doing it from thirty thousand feet above.

My dad and Mark's parents accompanied me on this unfamiliar journey to create a beautiful farewell for my Love. Mark's father and my dad were in the front seat of my father-in-law's Cadillac CTS, and my sweet mother-in-law and I were in the back seat. Flashback to the many times Mark and I either went to dinner or a movie with his parents with the same seating arrangement—boys in the front seat and girls in the back seat—Italian style is what his family called this! It was a beautiful fall day with the spectacular gold, orange, and red foliage amidst the brilliance of the sun. I reflected on all the times we were headed someplace with excitement, and was grateful for each and every one of those moments.

We arrived at Yur's Funeral Home in Geneva, IL. The same care and compassion I felt while they were at my home the previous night was present during this visit. We worked through all the details, signed paperwork, and then the moment came. The moment I never, in a million years, could have prepared for. This was my very first experience with funeral planning. The funeral director took me and my family into a room filled with caskets to select one for Mark.

Who. The. Frick. Knew?

There was a room filled with every type of casket you could imagine; cherrywood, mahogany, bronze, copper, walnut, pine, pewter. All I could think was "OH MY GOD, HOW IS THIS HAPPENING?" The same superpower I tapped into when these same people came to take Mark from our home kicked in. As much as I wanted to crumble, to fold, and to deny that this was my reality, I carried on. With grace. I selected a pewter casket for Mark. Pewter seemed appropriate for my Love, and it seemed protective, as odd as that may seem. It also reminded me of our wedding bands. We went back into the funeral director's office and solidified details. I brought Mark's suit and tie. I wanted Mark to have a white shirt rather than the blue one I brought, and the director took care of purchasing one. I had to select his prayer card with the saying on the back of it. I wanted it to be reflective of Mark, with words that would help all of us left behind to cope without him.

When I Must Leave You

> When I must leave you for a little while, please do not grieve or shed wild tears and hug your sorrow to you through the years. But start out bravely with a gallant smile, and for my sake in my name live on and do all things the same. Feed not your loneliness on empty days but fill each waking hour in useful ways. Reach out your hand in comfort and in cheer, and I in turn will comfort you and hold you near. And never, never be afraid to die, for I am waiting for you in the sky.

I decided to have his photograph from our wedding day on the prayer card. I know it was one of the happiest days in our life together. I added a caption at the bottom of the photograph, which embodied how I felt about Mark's fight with illness. I chose the verse from 2 Timothy 4:7: "I have competed well; I have finished the race; I have kept the faith" (NET Bible). Oh, what a race it was!

I had an appointment with Monsignor Knox at St. Patrick's church. Again, Dad came with me. Throughout this time, Dad was my rock. I was so blessed to have him walk beside me on my grief journey. Monsignor Knox wanted to know all about Mark from our perspective. At this time, I shared that I wanted to do his eulogy but was afraid that I would be too emotional. His advice to me was to pray about this and then make my decision.

The following day, my dad, Mark's parents, and I went to the cemetery. We drove there in our usual Italian-style placement; it was comforting, but then it wasn't. Mark was buried at a cemetery that is the final resting place of his grandparents and other relatives. The cemetery office was so ancient-looking, and their methods for locating an available plot were so very archaic. The woman trying to assist us seemed to be like a cartoon figure. She reminded me of Polly from *Underdog*, except the woman had dark black hair. We settled on a location and went to the site to visit. We decided on an outdoor crypt—I call it his high-rise. Mark's resting place is under the presence of St. Michael the Archangel. This was an experience where details were important—his mom asked that we include his picture on his crypt, and of course I did.

So, let's reflect on St. Michael the Archangel. St. Michael is not a saint—he is an angel. In fact, he is the leader of all angels and the army of God. St. Michael has four main responsibilities:

- To combat Satan
- To escort the faithful to heaven at the hour of their death
- To be a champion of all Christians and the church
- To call men from life to their heavenly judgment

It is NOT a coincidence that this was the location that was available for us to select. The hand of God was in this. Additionally, the fact that Mark's final resting place is St. Joseph's cemetery is all interwoven with our story.

Dad and I arrived home early evening, and my tribe had begun arriving to Chicago to support me—rather, carry me through the experience of saying goodbye to Mark. My dear college friend, Hope, insisted upon coming in. She is a sweet soul whom I actually had not seen in many years. She was a bridesmaid in our wedding and I in hers. She dropped everything and came to Chicago to help hold me up. Other relatives did the same and took the next available flight in; they included my brother, godmother, cousins, and my sweet goddaughter. This is where they elected to be, and I was so incredibly grateful. Their presence held me up and helped me to continue moving forward. Every fiber of my being wanted to ball up in a cocoon and not deal with anything that was relevant to planning and preparing to say my final farewell to Mark.

Despite the busy and emotionally draining day at the cemetery, I still had a few things to take care of prior to Mark's funeral on Thursday, October 12. First, I needed something to wear! Hope and I hopped in her rental car to go dress shopping. Oh, how I wished we would have been dress shopping for a fun occasion. I recall walking into Talbot's and telling the salesperson that I was looking for a dress to wear to my husband's funeral. It was important for me to set boundaries by stating this aloud . . . Deep down I knew I needed to hear the words in order to believe my reality. She kindly assisted me and said she would keep me in her prayers. Additionally, I needed to go to the funeral home to view Mark to make sure he was laid to rest to my satisfaction.

Our niece Jessica and her six-month-old baby Noah met Hope and I at the funeral home. For all intents and purposes, Jess was estranged from the rest of the family. For Mark and me, this situation had absolutely nothing to do with us, so we maintained our relationship. I felt it important for Jess to say her final farewell to her uncle, whom she loved and adored. However, it was not appropriate for her to attend his funeral as her presence would have been a distraction to

Mark's farewell. Jess was able to say her goodbye to Mark in person; I am grateful that she was able to do this. And I am grateful that I had the foresight to make this happen—it was important for both Jessica and me.

After I got back, only my parents and brother were at our home. It was time for me to put my thoughts on paper for the eulogy. I remember asking for silence as I needed it to write out my thoughts. Below is what I came up with and delivered the following day in his honor.

> My sweet husband and I met in June of 2001. We met the nontraditional way through Match.com.
>
> We quickly formed a rapport over the telephone and through email, and it really was a whirlwind.
>
> We met on June 23, 2001, and were engaged two months and one day later. We married the following year—to have a proper courtship (!)—on October 5, 2002. Last Thursday, we celebrated fifteen years of marriage.
>
> I searched my entire adult life to find my soulmate.
>
> I prayed the nine-day novena to St. Joseph frequently! The novena is said for nine days for anything you may desire, and then to let go and let God.
>
> My prayer was to find my husband, a partner for life. That prayer was answered when I met Mark.
>
> We enjoyed life together and had many of the same interests—except *Star Trek*!
>
> As most of you know, Mark's illness was lengthy, and each year we adjusted to what was our "normal."
>
> We lived our vows; we loved and honored each other.
>
> Through my husband's death, I've been able to see the Hand of God in our Union.

> The role of wife/caretaker wasn't an easy path, but despite the pain Mark felt during his last few years of his life, he really didn't complain.
>
> I was blessed to witness Mark's transition to Heaven and am grateful for that Holy experience.
>
> So, the man I prayed for and love is at peace now, and his suffering has ended.
>
> St. Joseph played another role in our union. He helped usher Mark to Heaven. As I have reflected on this, I know that Mark lived his life much like St. Joseph—he was kind, compassionate, and caring.

I awakened the next morning and simply could not believe what was ahead of me. Again, that superpower kicked in, and I just did what I needed to do—like a trooper. I showered, fixed my hair, put on my makeup, and dressed for my final time to get ready for Mark and I. As I reflect back on this morning, I am not certain of how I was able to keep myself together. Thank God for waterproof mascara.

Mom, Dad, my brother Jim, and I mingled in our home that morning getting ready for the day, drinking coffee with the unspoken reality of what was ahead. They carried me through this moment, and I am not sure I would have had the strength to get through this unthinkable time without their love and support.

I am someone who thrives on details when it comes to occasions—even if that "occasion" is the funeral of my beloved. I wanted the funeral to be held in our church rather than in a funeral home. Additionally, I did not want a prolonged evening wake with a mass and burial the following day.

I arranged for a harpist while guests gathered and arranged to have photo books of our life together on display. I simply did not have the energy to put picture boards together. My beautiful and talented cousins, Lisa and Rod, played guitar and sang the song "Mary Did You Know." I am not sure how they kept their composure, but their voices sounded like angels singing.

I recall going into my "manager mode" making sure that everything was going well and the setting was what I wanted it to be. Family and friends were arriving, and I was trying so hard to be gracious and welcoming. Out of the corner of my eye, I saw a group of people coming into the Church. I realized it was my work family. I was astounded by the outpouring of support and love from my colleagues. At that moment, I lost my shit. I think it was *that* moment that made me realize that *this* moment was in fact REAL.

I was the last to say farewell to Mark before the casket was closed. Closed. This is always *the most difficult* time for us earthly beings. It's the last time to physically see our loved one—ever. The superpower I came to rely upon kicked in and allowed me to maintain my composure. Frankly, I wanted to fold over and fall to the floor. I wanted to disappear. God gave me grace. The monsignor did a lovely job with his homily and the selected readings. He told stories about Mark that the family shared with him. Our very brave godson and his friend served as altar boys. Mark had a beautiful mass, and I was able to deliver his eulogy at the end of the service. Surprisingly, I was able to deliver my message gracefully and without an emotional breakdown.

After the funeral service, we went to lunch as they do in the Chicago area. Growing up in the South, I am accustomed to the after-funeral gathering at someone's home. I was still surrounded by family and friends, as we dined and shared stories about Mark. We dined at my brother-in-law's country club. I couldn't help but think about the previous celebrations we had there and the juxtaposition of this dining experience.

The following day, we had a private burial service. The reason we did not have all services in one day was because the cemetery is about forty-five miles from the church. Mark's mom, dad, brother and wife, and godfather and wife met me and my family at the funeral home. The cars followed behind the hearse. Because there were only a few of us, I did not set up a police escort. After we arrived, we were all gathering around while they took the casket from the hearse. The very moment the casket was pulled from the hearse, a monarch butterfly swooped down. Mark made good on his promise to me! I was overjoyed and sorrowful at the same time. Several of my family members gleefully acknowledged this butterfly. This was only the beginning of the many signs Mark would provide to me to let me know he would always be with me.

We went inside the chapel, and my angel cousins sang "Amazing Grace," and the priest said final blessings for Mark. After this, I had to share with all present the meaning of the butterfly swooping down as the casket was removed from the hearse. I shared with them Mark's promise that, from heaven, he would always protect me and I would know by the butterfly. What a gift he gave to me and our families. THIS was definitely a God moment.

We departed the chapel and went to Mark's final resting place on this sunny, brisk day. Suffice it to say, this was an incredibly emotional moment as we watched Mark's casket raised up to the crypt. My husband's body was being placed where I would never be able to embrace him again. Oh, this was so final. This was the final goodbye for our families. Nothing can really prepare anyone for this moment. I reached deep within and asked God to keep me upright.

That superpower I tapped into was the *grace* bestowed upon me from God. Grace continues to carry me, and I know that all will be well . . . even if it does not feel like it will be.

The Lord is close to the brokenhearted and saves those who are crushed in spirit.

Ps. 34:18 (NIV)

Farewell Illinois

My tribe slowly started heading back to their own lives. First, it was my brother, who headed back to New Orleans to join Mary—now my sister-in-law—for a trip they previously planned. He was so loving and supportive during this tough time, and I was thankful he was there with me. The next day, my godmother, cousins, and goddaughter headed back home. I was so grateful they traveled to Chicago to support me and say farewell to Mark. I recall my cousin Rod and I were hanging out on the deck to get fresh air. He told me that he explained to his young children that he was going to be in Chicago for Mark's funeral. He told his children that this is what family does for one another—they help support and give the deceased a proper send-off.

Life continued. Saying goodbye added to my overall sadness, but I still had my parents, my friend Hope, and my cousin Jenn with me through the weekend after burying Mark. Those ladies continued to support me and helped to get all my thank-you notes out to those who attended Mark's services. Who knew that money could be enclosed in sympathy cards? I surely did not, as this was not a practice where I grew up. I put those generous gifts toward Mark's burial expenses. Who the hell knew the cost of THAT?

The girls left a few days later, and then there were three: Mom, Dad, and me. The anxiety that I felt was overwhelming, as I knew I was so very close to being the last one standing in my home—OUR home—without my husband. I cried—no, I sobbed—and was unsure of exactly how I would be able to navigate my way through this. Dusk and into the darkness of nighttime were and still are my most difficult moments without Mark. Yes, I had my faith to lean on, but at this moment that seemed so far-fetched. Sure, I prayed for the strength to get me through, but that prayer would not bring my Love back.

Mom and Dad stayed an additional week. This gave me a bit of breathing space as I continued to envision what life would be like in my Mark-less home. Dad supported me with getting my finances in order, meeting with my banker, and closing accounts and such. Mainly, they both stayed there to love me and make sure that I was okay.

Nine days after we buried Mark, I took Mom and Dad to the airport. They really wanted me to go home with them so I could have some space from my empty home. The truth was that my emptiness would exist no matter where I was because Mark WAS my home and I was his. I knew this alone time would be a test for me, and I began anticipating it the week prior to their departure.

I planned a visit to the Morton Arboretum after dropping them off at the airport so that I could go to a place that had meaning for Mark and me. I found both comfort and sadness. I recalled so many visits we had there together—some when he was completely healthy, and most when he relied on a cane to get around or when we simply stayed in the car because he couldn't walk freely. I was besieged by BUTTERFLIES! He was with me, gently letting me know everything would be okay. Often when I was anxious or upset, Mark would say, "Baby everything is going to be okay." For us, "okay" meant everything will be fine, do not worry, do not stress, all will be well.

I soaked in the fresh air, enjoyed the warmth of the sun,

and curiously watched families enjoy their day together. I was in a bubble, alone, having to navigate this new world without my partner, and trying ever so hard to grasp my reality and at the same time wonder if this was real. I spent a few hours there and took pictures of the beautiful fall flowers and decorations—something that was familiar, as I had pictures from previous visits.

When it was time to go home, I knew this would be a big step for me to step inside of an empty home. I did it. I think it was these tiny moments of my new acclimation that I knew I *needed* to get under my belt to set my course for survival.

I entered the driveway, pulled my car into the garage, and turned the car off. I closed the garage, disarmed the alarm, and gingerly entered my home. Despite knowing to expect emptiness, I called out "Baby," a familiar greeting for Mark. I looked at the empty chair Mark used to sit in and sobbed. I wanted to be alone, but I needed people.

As much as I wanted to run to my in-laws' home, I just could not. I wanted to crawl into someone's lap, but it couldn't be theirs. I knew they were experiencing their own grief and sadness, and I did not want to make them feel like they needed to take care of me too.

My dear sweet neighbors, Toni and Bob, were my anchors during those weeks of acclimating to my new life as a widow. W.I.D.O.W. How hard it was to even *think* at the time, and still the status is hard for me to acknowledge. I was free to knock on their door or call them whenever I needed them. I was free to cry and express my raw grief. You see, Bob had also suffered the loss of his first wife, and he knew firsthand what I was experiencing. My sweet friend Toni is a child of God and was able to pray with me and for me to help give me the strength I needed to overcome the depth of my sadness.

I have often referred to them as my angels. I am blessed and grateful they were always there for me and helped support me. Sometimes I would join them for dinner, sometimes for a glass of wine, and other times for them to wipe away my tears. They had a box of tissues at the ready for me, and, oh boy, did I use them.

I settled into that first week at home—alone. I knew I would only be there for a week and then would be off to Orlando to meet my family for a previously planned trip to celebrate my mom's eighty-second birthday at our usual spot—Disney World. I knew this would be a familiar place to be cocooned by my family and to try to find some glimmer of being *with* the living.

It didn't matter if I was in Disney World, home, my car, or at Mass; grief remained in every cell of my body. The trip was a nice distraction, and of course I had my moments where I broke down. This was the very last vacation place Mark and I had together the previous year. There were certain places I had to avoid simply because the memories were too fresh. I was happy to be there to celebrate my mom and took comfort in being with my family, and we so enjoyed just being together. The death of someone you love makes each moment so deeply precious.

After a week in Orlando, I was back to the quiet home without Mark. Mark and I had an agreement that I would move back to my hometown in the New Orleans area if anything happened to him. I knew my next step was to contact my Realtor and start the process of putting the house on the market. Steve met me a few days later and brought all of the necessary paperwork and comp sales for the area, and made a few suggestions to make my home ready for showing. I signed the paperwork that I used to blindly follow Mark's lead on because this was his area of expertise. I knew this was the right move for me, but at the same time I doubted myself.

I let Steve, my Realtor, out through the front door. When I went back into the family room, I spotted a lemonhead candy on the rug at the foot of the sofa. I laughed out loud! THIS was Mark reassuring me that I made the right move. There was no way THAT candy had *just* been sitting there. Mark used to suck on lemonheads to help him with his constant dry mouth before he had the feeding tube. We had not seen a lemonhead in our home for about a year. Immediately, I settled into my decision and knew that I would be okay. Despite that magnificent sign, of course, I also buried St. Joseph in the yard to help me sell our home.

Steve listed my home the following day and requests for showings began rolling in. The very first couple that viewed our home put in an offer. They offered about $15,000 less than my asking price. I recall talking to my Realtor and saying, "No, Steve, I want full asking price." He and I went back and forth for a bit, and after, I reminded him that this was the very first offer with four other requested showings and I would not settle.

Inside, I could not believe I was negotiating like this. Mark had always handled matters like this. His background in banking and his smarts on negotiation skills was his "job," and now here I was doing it without him. But was I? I got a call back from Steve: my counteroffer was accepted, and they wanted to take possession in December. My home sold in one day—Whoa, Nelly! This was moving way too quickly. I knew this quick time frame would not work, so I pushed back and we agreed on closing on January 22. Mark was keeping up his promise to always protect me—even if it was from Heaven.

The months that followed entailed preparing for a move back to the New Orleans area, including finding a home there, going through Mark's clothes, and wrapping my head around how fast all of this was happening. My faith in God, my belief that Mark was walking this journey with me, and the love and support from my family and friends kept me going.

By mid-November, I returned to work. I was happy to be back with my work family, as I could not ask for a better group of people to support me. I had tough days, and leaned on a few trusted colleagues to help me work through those moments of grief when I couldn't make the tears stop or when something triggered me. My core group listened, allowed me to cry on their shoulder, and gave me the space I needed to acclimate back to functioning at work. It was not easy, but I was supported, cared for, and grateful for my team.

I've often heard it said that major decisions should not be made within the first year following the death of a spouse. I am here to tell you that while that is good advice, it is only advice. There is no one-size-fits-all way to living a life without your person. My heartfelt advice is that all of us need to do what is best for US—in any situation.

One of the biggest and saddest hurdles that I faced was going through Mark's clothes and belongings. His mom and dad helped me with this most difficult process. I cannot even imagine what these two sweet souls were thinking. This was my husband, the man I loved with all my heart, BUT this was their SON. Parents should simply NOT have to deal with this. They were amazingly supportive (not surprising), and we went through it together. It was sad, we each had our moments, but we did what we needed to do—just like Mark would have wanted.

I am ever grateful for the wonderful times Mark and I shared with his parents and family. We enjoyed going to his parents' home for Sunday football and Cubs games in the summer, and we genuinely enjoyed doing things together.

My sweet neighbors asked for a favorite shirt of Mark's, and they would be making something special with it. No questions asked, I gave them one of his beloved polo shirts.

My sweet cousin and friend Jenn flew to Chicago to help support me while my home was packed up and to drive 981 miles from St. Charles, IL, to my new home in Louisiana. My in-laws gave me a beautiful send-off. It was all so sad but sweet at the same time. How do you say goodbye to two young boys who were loved so much by their uncle? I felt like they were now missing an aunt and an uncle.

It was so hard to say goodbye to my little support system of family, Toni, Bob, Maggie the nurse, and other dear friends. But I knew this was the direction I needed to go, and it would have been difficult to stay in OUR home.

Jenn and I hit the road for New Orleans on January 20, 2018, said a few more goodbyes, and soon my hometown for the past seventeen years was in the rearview mirror. My Jeep was loaded with the fragile and important treasures that I wanted to keep with me. We had a sunny and cold day, and I couldn't help but recall a few road trips that Mark and I had taken together to my hometown for fun. This trip was far from fun, but I had the love and support I needed as we traveled through the familiar countryside Mark and I once drove together.

We traveled through Illinois, Missouri, Arkansas, Tennessee, Mississippi, and finally Louisiana. The weather changed from mid-thirties, sunny, and chilly with brownish grass to warmer temperatures and greener grass the further south we drove. When we hit the Louisiana state line, a picture time-stamping this moment was important to me. I think it made the whole situation real for me.

This move was remarkably different than all the moves I have been through. In the past, moves were filled with excitement for the unknown and what was to come. This move was bittersweet, as I left behind a life I loved so much with the man I adored, yet I was headed home to familiarity, family, and friends.

I settled in with my parents for a few days while my furniture and belongings were en route to my new home. I found comfort being in my childhood home with Mom and Dad, but still struggled to come to terms with my new reality . . . life without my Froggie.

My command is this: Love each other as I have loved you.

John 15:12 (NIV)

Commitment

THERE WERE TIMES WHERE IT would have been easy to walk away. It would have been easy to pack up and move back to New Orleans. It would have been easy to simply take care of myself. Yes, there were times when I simply did not know if I had it in me to maintain my commitment to my husband. During those times, I was exhausted or frustrated because our path did not go in the direction we had planned.

I was pissed off that Mark had to suffer in pain and that I had to watch from the sidelines, unable to do anything for him to take away the pain.

I was unapologetically angry that this kind man had to endure so much. He simply could not catch a break. It always seemed like it was one thing after another—one setback after another.

He never complained.

There were times I would fall on my knees with my head on his lap as he sat in his chair. I sobbed for the loss of our life we were supposed to build together. He would stroke my hair and lovingly rub my back with his contorted fingers. His words for me were always (and I mean always) "It will be okay; everything will be okay."

It was NOT.

Our inability to conceive a child was gut-wrenching for both of us, but Mark taught me how to accept the hand that we were dealt. He taught me to be grateful for what we DID have—each other. That was a lesson to help prepare both of us for what was to come.

During his last year, we had more trips to the hospital via ambulance than I can count or even care to recall. I remember that sheer feeling of helplessness. There were countless days I would arrive at the hospital well before seven a.m. to meet with doctors and the medical team and spend all day working from the hospital. I would drag myself to the car late at night and drive home. It was dark, I was alone, and I was going inside of our empty home. As I drove the car into the garage, I would always close the garage door as soon as I pulled in.

Occasionally, deep down inside, I thought if I just remained in my car with it still running, with the garage door pulled shut, I would simply fall asleep and all of my pain and sadness would be over. As quickly as the thought entered, it left. Sometimes, it frightened me to have this random thought pop in my head. I wondered, "Why him—why us? Why, God, were you doing this to him? To us?"

I am human, and it is okay that I felt those moments of weakness. I was a faithful wife to my husband, Mark, and we lived our vows.

How were we able to accomplish this?

FAITH.

PURE.

BLIND.

FAITH.

My faith is what allowed me to hang on. By the sheer grace of God, I was able to maintain my full-time job and be a full-time caregiver to Mark.

Early on in his illness, I would work all day and then stay awake through the night while he slept to research his condition or review medical reports. In the last year of his life, there were days that I was so exhausted, I would fall asleep behind the wheel of the car as I drove home from a business trip. There were nights when all I was able to do was nap because I had to take care of Mark's medications or help him to the bathroom. There were times when Mark was so frustrated that he had to rely on me to take care of him and moments when communication just took too much effort.

There were days when I pushed him to see another doctor or take another test. Anything to help him recover and get better.

As I reflect on our marriage, I know that our union was not happenstance. This was the man I fell in love with as we got to know one another over the telephone and via email . . . same for him. I would say *that* is unbridled faith we had in each other. We took a leap, determined to share a life with one another. Illness was not part of the plan but a course we had no control over.

Sure, my belief in God was shaken to the core, and there were years where it was hard for me to be a child of God. There were times of doubt, confusion, and anger that WE had to endure this reality. On the rare occasion, we would talk about this hand we'd been dealt. Sometimes Mark would say, "What did I do to deserve this?" or "God must hate me." Always, and I mean always, no matter how I was feeling, I would reassure him that this was not a punishment from God. He would respond back with "I don't know what I did to make Him mad." Again, I delved deep into my faith reservoir and tried my hardest to assure him that he did not do anything.

Sometimes, I thought my own human mistakes were the cause of what was happening to us. There were times where my actions caused pain to others, and was this the price for that? Deep within, I always knew that my God is not a punishing God and that I had been forgiven of those human mistakes—I was always taught that since I was a child.

Despite the days that I wanted to run away—hop in my Jeep and drive west until I hit the ocean—I chose to honor our commitment to love in sickness and in health. Was I afraid? Yes. Was I surrounded by a loving and supportive family? Yes. Did Mark deserve this? Hell, no. I stayed for him and for us because we needed each other.

Marriage is a covenant and is a commitment that God initiates, and my duty was to love in sickness and in health. When I looked at my reality through that lens, I became acutely aware that our union was formed for a purpose. We had some lovely times together as a married couple and also some trying times that ripped us to our core. But we survived the difficulty *together*.

Commitment to each other, no matter the circumstances, was the glue that held us together. My primary goal was to always care for Mark in a way that made him feel loved and not a burden. Sure, there were times he did feel like that. There were times I felt like I couldn't give any more, but I always found the strength to show love and compassion even when I was discouraged and sad.

There were times that I pushed him to see another doctor or continue with some sort of therapy or even entertain me and try acupuncture. Simply put, I wanted him to have a decent quality of life. Mark mostly went along with my thoughts, sometimes pushed back, but in the end, he showed his commitment to us to try something. Then there were times where we lay in bed next to each other and locked eyes without words spoken, and we knew. We knew we were perfectly fit to be there for each other in the capacity that both of us had within to give . . . to each other.

I was Mark's wife for 5483 days, 1 hour, and 36 minutes, and he taught me so much during our journey. Mark was brave, and he taught me to be brave even when I didn't think I had the capacity for bravery. He was kind, and he taught me that kindness is a joyful and simple way to live. Mark taught me the importance of slowing down and enjoying just being. Our best days were those that were simple—hanging at home, catching a movie (he was such a movie buff!), taking a Sunday drive, or hitting the local pool. With our inability to have children, he taught me how to cope with life when our dreams are not realized.

Through his death, Mark has taught me that although he isn't with me physically, he is always with me in spirit, and I am never without him.

Blessed are those who mourn, for they shall be comforted.

Matthew 5:4 (NASB)

Life without My Love

I SETTLED INTO MY NEW HOME. It is so odd to be in a home with OUR stuff. My bedroom is in the exact order of the bedrooms from our past two homes. Sometimes when I am lying in bed, I close my eyes and imagine Mark is right there next to me. Then I open my eyes and reality sets in.

It is said that the year of firsts is so difficult as grievers navigate through those anniversary dates of their loved one. Because my Sweetheart was ill for an extended period of time, my grief began years prior to his actual death. I mourned the loss of our marriage, of our ability to golf together, of our ability to travel without a wheelchair or scooter, of our ability to make love, and I even mourned that we could not have dinner at our kitchen table or cook together.

I am not sure if it is easier to be the widow of a spouse who had an extended illness or to be the widow of a spouse who died suddenly. Either scenario is difficult. Either scenario sucks. My perspective changed after Mark's death. The things that were always a big deal at work and life seemed insignificant.

I plugged along during that first year. I spent time with family and friends and sometimes savored being alone. I looked for those God moments to reassure me that all would be well. I wrote a Facebook entry on the ninth day of every month. Every ninth on the calendar triggered sadness for me, and I relived each hour of the ninth of October, when my

Love went to Heaven. Even now, it still happens.

October 9, 2017: I shared Mark's obituary. It was surreal: "I'm heartbroken but know my sweetheart is at peace. Please keep our family in your prayers during this time. AILYS, my Prince."

The first month of life went by, and most days it was hard to breathe. I remember a trip I took during this time. I was people watching from the time I pulled up to the departures lane and watched couples embracing as they said their goodbyes. I watched families scurry out of cars, squealing with excitement for their upcoming trip. The long kisses, long goodbyes tore at my heart.

As I sat in the United Club lounge, I found myself trying to make sense of my new reality. I journaled the following:

> Here's what I do know . . . Mark and I loved each other for 15 years and 4 days and told each other I love you every single one of those days. I miss him, but I have to remember he is at PEACE. God, help me to adjust to life without my sweet Mark.

November 9, 2017:

> It's odd . . . sometimes my thought is that the world should stop.
>
> Mark is missed by so many, and his life on Earth was too short.
>
> Blessed and grateful to have loved and been loved.
>
> One month ago today, my Sweetheart went to Heaven.
>
> Miss you, Froggie

My first December without Mark was incredibly difficult. Mark was Mr. Christmas. Yes, he was the guy who would start watching "Christmas in July" Hallmark movies. And yes, I poked fun at him for doing so! We would always decorate the Christmas tree the day after Thanksgiving, and we went all out. The tree was huge, about ten feet tall, and had LED lights that gave us the option of all-white lights or colored lights. He loved shopping for my gift, and he could never keep his surprise a secret! He couldn't wait to exchange gifts.

When he was younger, he would always select one person in his family to get an extra-special gift. He took great delight in giving to others, and this started at an early age. Every Christmas Eve, we left milk and cookies for Santa and read "'Twas the Night Before Christmas." Each Christmas morning, he insisted we take goofy pictures with our gifts to each other. Those were simple and special times and I treasure those sweet memories.

December 9, 2017:

> A friend made this sweet bear from Mark's polo shirt.
>
> Missing my sweetheart and asking for prayers for strength.

I spent my first Christmas in St. Charles. It was important for me to be with Mark's family for my first Christmas—they were my connection to him. Additionally, I thought of our nephews and didn't want them to have two empty seats at the Christmas dinner table. I spent Christmas Eve and Christmas Day with my in-laws. I absolutely did not want to be in our home alone. We attended Christmas Eve Mass and had a low-key Christmas Eve. Christmas Day was filled with all of our usual traditions, but this time it also included a big hole in our heart—the absence of Mark, a son, husband, brother, and uncle.

This was my journal entry during that time:

> Am I going to be okay? Of course you will, tap into your inner strength.
>
> When will this hole go away? Never—it won't feel as vast.
>
> So much has happened since 9/30/17—the day you went to the hospital for the last time.
>
> I miss you every single day.
>
> I do find it much harder to be home where we used to live together.
>
> Missing you so much.
>
> So much sadness in my soul.
>
> I need you to continue to be with me to help me have strength.
>
> *AILYS*, MST
>
> [Forever seems too long to be without you.]

I flew to New Orleans for New Year's Eve. My mom broke her hip in early December and was in a rehabilitative facility healing. Dad and I spent the evening with her, and we had Chinese food for dinner in honor of Mark. Every New Year's Eve, our tradition was to enjoy Veuve Clicquot and order Chinese food. We savored being tucked away in our home on such a high-energy night. For us, just being together, reflecting on the year that was slipping away, and anticipating a new one was perfect. Typically, we watched the ball drop in New York City to have countdown for the eastern standard time zone, and we would have lights out when the clock actually struck midnight in our central standard time zone.

January 9, 2018:

> Froggie
>
> Pup
>
> Baby
>
> Markus
>
> Kooch
>
> Bubba (my Southern nickname for him)
>
> Marky Mark
>
> All of the above were pet names for my Sweetheart.
>
> So very hard to believe he left me 3 months ago.
>
> Too much change in too little time.
>
> However, he's with me and guiding me along the way.
>
> Nothing has been a coincidence.
>
> *AILYS*, Mark Trimarco

By February 9, I had relocated back to the New Orleans area and reacclimated with family and friends, trying to find my rhythm in this new life. I posted a few inspiring pictures with sweet quotes:

> 4 short months ago today, you went to Heaven.
>
> I miss you and love you with all my heart.
>
> *AILYS*

Early that year, I began searching for support groups to help me cope with my grief. I went to my church and spoke to one of the priests. They didn't have anything available there, and he referred me to a local funeral home where they had a speaker series for people grieving. I wasn't up for going to that sort of setting. I found GriefShare, a national recovery support group that meets for thirteen weeks. I attended a few meetings when I was able, based on my travel for work. I recall one of the meetings was only attended by another lady and me. She found her son dead of an apparent overdose, and my heart immediately went out to her. By being part of this group, my focus was on others instead of myself. It was helpful but still a struggle.

March 9, 2018:

> I couldn't help but notice that on this same day, in 2015, I posted the following:
>
>> *Be soft.*
>>
>> *Do not let the world make you hard.*
>>
>> *Do not let the pain make you hate.*
>>
>> *Do not let the bitterness steal your sweetness.*
>>
>> *Take pride that even though the rest of the world may disagree, you still believe it to be a beautiful place.*
>>
>> —Iain Thomas
>
> Who knew Mark wouldn't be here then.
>
> He suffered and was ill but never really believed he'd leave us.
>
> We all miss him and remember his big heart.
>
> Only 5 months ago, you went to Heaven.
>
> Seems like yesterday and yet it seems like a lifetime ago.
>
> I won't let my loss make me hardened, bitter, or allow the pain to make me hate.

> I will continue to ebb and flow and figure out how to carry on.
>
> *AILYS*, Mark

I planned a vacation that month. I went to Sedona to get away in hopes of giving myself some space to heal. My goal was to be in a serene setting with nature, and I wasn't disappointed. It was a beautiful and spiritual experience. I stayed at Mii amo, a spa resort, and was pampered and taken care of beyond my expectations! Loved my time there hiking, spa-ing, swimming, and doing yoga. It was both relaxing and therapeutic. After so many years of caretaking, this time to connect with myself was important.

My journal entry the day of my trip:

> First solo vacation. Miss you baby.
>
> I'm overly indulging for this trip—just felt I needed a break in a big way.
>
> With the many years of Mark's illness, the stress, exhaustion on November 2016–October 9, 2017, I simply needed to decompress.
>
> Buried my husband
>
> Sold my house
>
> Went through all of Mark's cothes/belongings
>
> Downsized
>
> Moved to another state
>
> Mom broke her hip in December
>
> Traveling for work on a weekly basis
>
> To say I have been through a lot of change is an understatement.

Expectations for this trip:

- decompress
- immerse myself in the moment
- experience everything I can
- grieve
- be okay with my grief
- connect with my soul to begin understanding how this story—this love story—is supposed to be told
- enjoy myself
- be kind to myself
- rejuvenate
- journal

AILYS, MST

Can't believe you're not here

The trip was everything I wanted and needed it to be. I was pampered, relaxed, and came home rejuvenated. But I still felt it was important for me to get into grief therapy. I ran into a friend who suggested a grief therapist, and I thought I would give that a try. She and I met for two sessions. I recall entering her office for the first time: it was a pleasant and comfortable environment. During our first session, I told her my story and all that was involved with Mark's illness and my caretaking. I recall talking about resilience and being mindful and not judging myself... That it was okay to feel bad. She reinforced that grief is a process.

I met her a second time a few weeks later. We discussed how things were going and how I was feeling. It was apparent to me that we were not connecting. At the end of the session, we had about a two-minute stare down, and in that time she didn't have anything to say to me, nor did I to her. It was as if she felt like I was doing well since she told me I was doing great. What the hell?! On the inside I was dying, and this—excuse my language—bitch said I was doing great?

Please. I broke up with her over text.

The next few months, I plugged along. I had days and nights of deep depression and sadness. I continued working and trying to cope. It was not easy, but each day I put one foot in front of the other. I was so grateful to be with my parents, family, and friends, but I struggled with my deep loss. Mark wasn't with me. He isn't with me. It was so very hard to wrap my head around that. I think I was numb.

April 9, 2018:

> *AILYS*, my heart Mark Trimarco
>
> 6 months ago today you earned your wings.
>
> I love and miss you. I know I was one of the blessed ones to find my soul mate and my true love.
>
> Keep protecting me, from Heaven, Love . . . just like you promised.

An exerpt from my April journal entry:

> I feel like something within has shifted. I look around and you are not here with me. I am using the same utensils, dinnerware, the same everything, and it feels so surreal—in a completely different home and state. Frequently, I look for you, and you are not here.
>
> Last week was a horrible week of sadness, with lots of tears . . .
>
> My shift internally feels like strength—feels like grace. My inner voice is telling me I'm going to be okay. I hear you saying everything is going to be okay like you always did when I couldn't pull it together . . . I need to plan my own option B. That plan includes telling our story . . .
>
> *AILYS*, M

And I Love You So

May 9, 2018:

> My sweet Mark Trimarco.
>
> Today marks 7 months since you went to Heaven.
>
> Miss you, love you, and am grateful to have your unconditional love.
>
> The mold was broken afer you joined our lives.
>
> *AILYS,* M

May 19 was Mark's first birthday in Heaven. It was important for me to honor his day, so I had a Mass celebrated in his honor and threw a celebration of his life. I invited family and friends to join me in remembering Mark on his birthday. We dined on some of his favorite foods—seafood, dips, and yellow cake with chocolate frosting. We released balloons, and I said a prayer just before we cut the cake. It was a special day and a nice way for me to handle my grief in a productive way. Believe me, there was a nanosecond when I thought I could just remain in bed all day and skip May 19 entirely . . . but I didn't. It was important for me to show myself that I could survive this sad first.

That first summer was really rough for me. I battled depression so terribly but continued to work and try to maintain my life. At one point, I phoned my Employee Assistance Program and was placed on hold for seven minutes. I hung up, dialed back in, and told the person on the other end of the phone it was a good thing I wasn't suicidal since I was placed on hold for too long. She told me there was a different number for that. I was done. I reached out to my godmother, who put me in touch with a remarkable grief therapist, who has and continues to help me tremendously.

I have learned through this process that my grief will

always be with me, and I will learn how to cope with the low times and savor the peaceful times. Grief is not linear, and the most unique things can set me off. Every day I awaken to my day without my Love, and every day I have a choice—to carry on or fold. Some days I carry on, and some days I fold. And some days are a dance with carrying on and folding. And it is okay.

In June of 2018, I had a very early-morning flight from New Orleans to Chicago. I was in my usual window seat, my seatmate was in the aisle seat, and I breathed a sigh of relief that the middle seat was empty. It was early. I had my earbuds in and plugged away working on my laptop. I noticed the lady (my seatmate) was praying the rosary. We did not speak at all during the flight as I was working and she was praying. We exchanged a few smiles and acknowledged one another, but did not speak.

As we touched down, I noticed she had a lanyard on that had Medjugorje on it. Medjugorje is a town in Bosnia and Herzegovina where the Blessed Mother appears to give messages to her followers. I actually went there in the late '80s with my parents on a pilgrimage. After we arrived at the gate and everyone was getting their luggage down, I noticed her husband, who was seated in the aisle row on the opposite side, took their luggage down from the overhead bin. There was a butterfly luggage tag smiling at me.

Since I had already noticed both the rosary and the lanyard, I felt comfortable chatting with this lovely lady (not that I am opposed to chatting on a flight, but I knew this conversation was about to get deep). I commented on the butterfly luggage tag and then told her my butterfly story. I opened up to a complete stranger about the death of my husband and the promise from him to always protect me even from Heaven.

She immediately disclosed that she had been praying for

me. Surprisingly, I asked why. I say "surprisingly" because when I'm in a moment like that, it isn't typical to ask for details—at least not for me. She told me she sensed sadness. We spoke for a bit, and then she pointed to the luggage tag and said, "There's your butterfly moment." She told me she and her husband were headed to Rome and then to Medjugorje. We wished each other well. When I got off the plane, I saw her waiting for others in her party. We hugged for such a long time. I told her she was my angel.

I have been blessed with many God moments to help me stay connected to Mark and to our story; I am blessed.

June 9, 2018:

> 8 months ago today you went to Heaven, my sweet Marky.
>
> Grateful for the many signs you show me along the way.
>
> You promised to protect me from Heaven; you always kept your promises.
>
> Thank you.
>
> *AILYS*

July 9, 2018: the Facebook posting was in response to a beautiful song about losing a loved one:

> Simply beautiful.
>
> And oh so fitting.
>
> Today is nine months from the day my Sweetheart went to Heaven.
>
> These past few days have been especially difficult.

> Our Markie is in Heaven, and he is keeping watch over all of us.

AILYS

I was in Chicago in early August and wanted to visit the cemetery and leave flowers at Mark's final resting place. My Facebook posting:

> Visited the cemetery today.
>
> 10 short months ago, you earned your wings, Mark.
>
> It's indescribable how much I miss you.

AILYS

August is my birthday month. My very first one without my Love. My last birthday with Mark on Earth was sad—we couldn't celebrate like we typically do. Normally we would have dined out, but due to Mark's feeding tube, that wasn't an option. Instead his mom took me to a beautiful lunch while his dad stayed with him.

I purchased tickets for my parents and me to see Tony Bennett, who performed at the Saenger Theatre on the night of my birthday. Mark and I had seen him perform in Chicago, and we enjoyed his timeless songs. Our seats were about seven rows from the stage on the right. There was an empty seat next to me. If you know anything about New Orleans, you never meet a stranger—everyone talks with one another. I greeted the woman seated to the left of the empty seat, and we quickly formed a rapport. She explained she purchased a ticket for her friend who was unable to attend the show because her son-in-law was in the hospital.

As the conversation continued, I shared that it was my

birthday, and she offered well-wishes. I added that it was my first one without my husband. She kindly expressed her sorrow to learn of this. I shared with her that we were married fifteen years and four days, and gave her a little of our story. It was an easy conversation about the loss of my husband, but it wasn't a sad conversation. She told me that I was very fortunate to have experienced the depth of love we shared and that not everyone is that lucky. Those words struck me. I do not think I was lucky; I am blessed. In the middle of the performance, she leaned over to me and said, "Your husband is with you," and glanced at the empty seat. To me, this is another God moment—where Mark is present with me even if he isn't here physically. His love will always be with me. What are the odds of an empty seat, front orchestra, at a sold-out performance?

September 9, 2018: another cemetery visit:

Earlier in the year, I was looking for a friend of mine who happened to be a priest. I wanted to know where he was serving and which mass he was saying on that particular Saturday night. I ended up using Google to help me research, and quickly learned that Father Steve was leading a pilgrimage to the Holy Land in October 2018. The dates EXACTLY coincided with the first anniversary of Mark's death and our first anniversary that he wasn't with me on Earth. And the frosting on the cake: Father Steve was part of our wedding ceremony where he was a musician.

How could this even be planned? This was a God sign. I leapt at the chance to go to Israel, to the Holy Land, where Jesus walked to be close to God and to Mark. What better way than to go with the priest leading the pilgrimage that knew me AND knew Mark. I signed up. I had something to look forward to, and I had something to be excited about—even in the midst of my sadness.

I traveled from New Orleans to Tel Aviv to spend time in the holiest place to help me continue my own unique grief journey. We traveled to Tiberias on the Sea of Galilee. We visited Mount Tabor—scene of the Transfiguration of Christ—

And I Love You So

St. Joseph's Church, and Mary's Well.

I met some wonderful people on my pilgrimage who were very supportive during this emotionally and faith-filled experience. On our anniversary, I was in Cana. Cana of Galilee! To Christians, Cana is known as the place where Jesus performed his first public miracle, turning water into wine at a wedding feast when the wine ran out. The couples on the pilgrimage renewed their wedding vows. It was beautiful and sad at the same time. But how blessed I was to be at this sacred place on what would have been our sixteen-year wedding anniversary. I was able to reflect on our union and praise God for uniting us.

We traveled to Haifa, Mount Carmel, Caesarea Maritima, and then to the Holy City of Jerusalem. We also went to Church of the Nativity, which stands upon the site where Jesus was born, visited the birthplace of St. John the Baptist and the Church of Visitation, where Mary visited her cousin Elizabeth and proclaimed the Magnificat.

On the anniversary of Mark's death, we visited Pater Noster, where Jesus taught his disciples the Lord's Prayer. I did the readings for mass on that day. My Facebook posting on the Anniversary of Mark's death captures this day:

> One year ago today, you went to be with Our Father.
>
> How appropriate that we had mass today at Pater Nastor where Jesus taught His disciples to pray the Our Father.
>
> *AILYS* sweet Mark
>
> We miss you, we love you, and appreciate the gift of signs you provide

We went to the Garden of Gethsemane, where Jesus prayed his last prayer before his arrest.

I was so blessed to carry the cross as we retraced the last steps of Jesus along the Via Dolorosa (Way of Sorrow) and as we walked through the markets of the Old City and prayed the Stations of the Cross. We went to the Church of the Holy Sepulchre, the church built on the site of Jesus' Crucifixion and burial. We also went to the Wailing Wall and left prayers tucked inside the wall.

Our last day was spent in Bethany, where we renewed our baptismal vows in the Jordan River. To walk amongst the sites I had only heard about on Sundays at Mass or in religion classes was beyond surreal. We ended our day in the Dead Sea—the lowest point on Earth. We were able to float in the sea! The sea is so high in salt content that you float.

What a sacred journey for me to walk with Jesus in my time of suffering and sadness and to know that Mark and I will be united again in Heaven. I am humbled and blessed to have walked where Jesus did. Along the way, there were many butterflies that reminded me of Mark's love for me and my love for him. I was greeted by a butterfly on every single stop we made. In one of the last conversations we had, he told me I would know he was with me when there were butterflies.

My love for Mark is deep, and I firmly believe our union was orchestrated by the hand of God. He brought two people together who fell in love sight unseen because He knew we needed each other to have and to hold . . . till death do us part.

My overarching goal is to continue to walk my grief journey with grace. Ultimately, I want to help others who are faced with loss, and minister to them as someone who has been there. I have hope for my future and know Mark is proud of the life I am living. I know I am.

And I Love You So . . . always.

Acknowledgments

Without Mark, I would not have experienced what it truly means to love and be loved. Mark's kind heart and big brown eyes were a mirror to help me love myself. He was my home—a feeling oh so comfortable that I could have sworn we knew each other an eternity. Through his illness, he was brave, rarely complained, and taught me to enjoy the moment. Thank you, My Love, for keeping your promise to me.

During periods of my life, I have journaled, but it was never a regular habit. I found myself journaling during Mark's last year and as I began my life as a widow. Putting words on paper was a way to help me process my new reality. Shortly after Mark went to Heaven, I knew I needed to figure out a way to tell our story. I was intentional about my healing trips to Sedona and Jerusalem to help me formulate my plan.

I don't recall exactly when I began following Gen Georget, but in early March 2019, I saw a post that spoke very loudly to me. It was entitled "Ridiculously Long Post Alert," and the gist of it was to do what you feel called to do despite fear.

Ridiculously Long Post Alert

> And I don't share this story with you to show what I can do. I share this story with you to show what letting go can do.

> I share this story to show what God can do.
>
> When we let Him.
>
> Let me say that again: WHEN WE LET HIM.
>
> I believe, with every fiber of my being, that it's impossible to move forward when fear is holding you back.
>
> I believe, from the core of my soul, that the moment I let go was the same moment that I opened myself up.
>
> I believe, with every ounce of my truth, that there is power beyond measure in the act of surrender.
>
> And I also believe that it can be one of the hardest things for us as humans to do.
>
> I want to dedicate this day to you.
>
> To releasing your fear. To owning your courage. To finding your freedom.
>
> I dedicate this day to letting the chains fall.

In that very moment, I let my chains fall. My chains of uncertainty, terror, and the unknown were released and ready to explore. I sent Gen a DM, and we exchanged a few messages back and forth.

This amazing and talented soul was placed in my path and cheering me on before we ever met! So, Gen, thank you from the bottom of my heart for being there and leading me to the finish line. Our relationship began with you as my writing coach, and now I am blessed to call you my friend. You pushed me to share what was in my heart and helped guide me along this rapid journey.

To my mom, dad, and brother, Jim, my little nuclear family. You all have been with me through the great times and the trying times, and I am blessed to call you my family. Your unwavering support means the world to me. I love you.

To Mark's parents and my forever in-laws, Patt and Mike. Your love and support throughout the good and tough times means more than I can ever say.

Also, I would be remiss if I did not acknowledge the fact that every single time I sat down to write, the music of Lorraine Hess was always playing in the background. I took great comfort in the song she wrote for her son and his wife for their marriage, "By Grace"; the lyrics spoke to me. Couples enter the covenant of marriage knowing vows include "in sickness and in health, for richer or for poorer, until death do us part." However, the reality of those sacred vows is not *if* but *when*. For Mark and me, our union ended before either of us ever wanted, and the reality of the work, effort, and love that goes into a "not so perfect happily ever after" is not for the faint of heart. Lorraine's music helped center me and receive the work of God as I told our story.

> By grace, our covenant is sealed by God.
>
> By grace, we'll serve each other faithfully.
>
> By grace, we'll build a family that prays and forgives.
>
> By grace . . . all will be well.
>
> For better, for worse,
>
> For rich or for poor,
>
> In sickness and health,
>
> 'Til death do us part.
>
> We're able to love because God loved us first.
>
> By God's grace, all will be well.

Excerpt from "By Grace," by Lorraine M. Hess, copyright © 2017, World Library Publications, wlpmusic.com. All rights reserved. Used by permission.

To my RTC family, thank you for helping my vision become a reality.

To my extended family, colleagues, and many friends who have helped keep me upright, I love you all.

Finally, I thank the good Lord above for selecting Mark to be my husband and for giving us the grace and strength we needed throughout our journey. He knew we needed each other. So thankful for all of the ways He shows up in my life each day.

My hope is that this glimpse into our journey can help others in a similar situation. My ultimate desire is to help others walk their grief journey and to help those entering the sacrament of marriage understand that there will be times that are beyond the scope of what we're prepared to handle.

And with God, all things are possible.

Love & light,
Melanie

Biography

I am a widow.

This is a descriptor I never would have dreamed would be attached to me at such a relatively young age.

But I am.

I grew up in the New Orleans area and was surrounded by a loving family, friends, and I am blessed to have a firm foundation in my Catholic faith. Little did I know in my early days how much I would come to rely on that faith.

I never—and I mean EVER—dreamed the word "author" would be attached to my name.

After the death of my sweet husband, I knew I needed to share our story. The purpose was two-fold, and I was only cognizant of one aspect as I thought through this goal.

Firstly, I wanted to share our story to help others who may be walking their grief journey. Additionally, I wanted to highlight the importance of commitment—it's easy to walk away in today's world. Walking away from a commitment isn't always the best response.

Secondly, the act of putting pen to paper was amazingly cathartic for me. Of course, there were some very tough moments to relive. I know that it helped me to realize that both of us did the very best we could while embarking this journey "in sickness." I had no idea how healing this experience would be for me as I grieved the loss of my Love.

As a child of God, I continue to seek the ways He is using me to share my experience of love and loss to help minister to others.

Our world was brighter when Mark was here, but we all strive to keep his memory alive.

Melanie was born and raised in New Orleans, Louisiana, to Marilyn and Jim Baker, her parents whom she is grateful to be living nearby. Her brother, Jim, and his wife, Mary, are also in the area and are tremendous support.

Melanie frequently spends time with Mark's parents, and finds great comfort in this connection to them and to Mark.

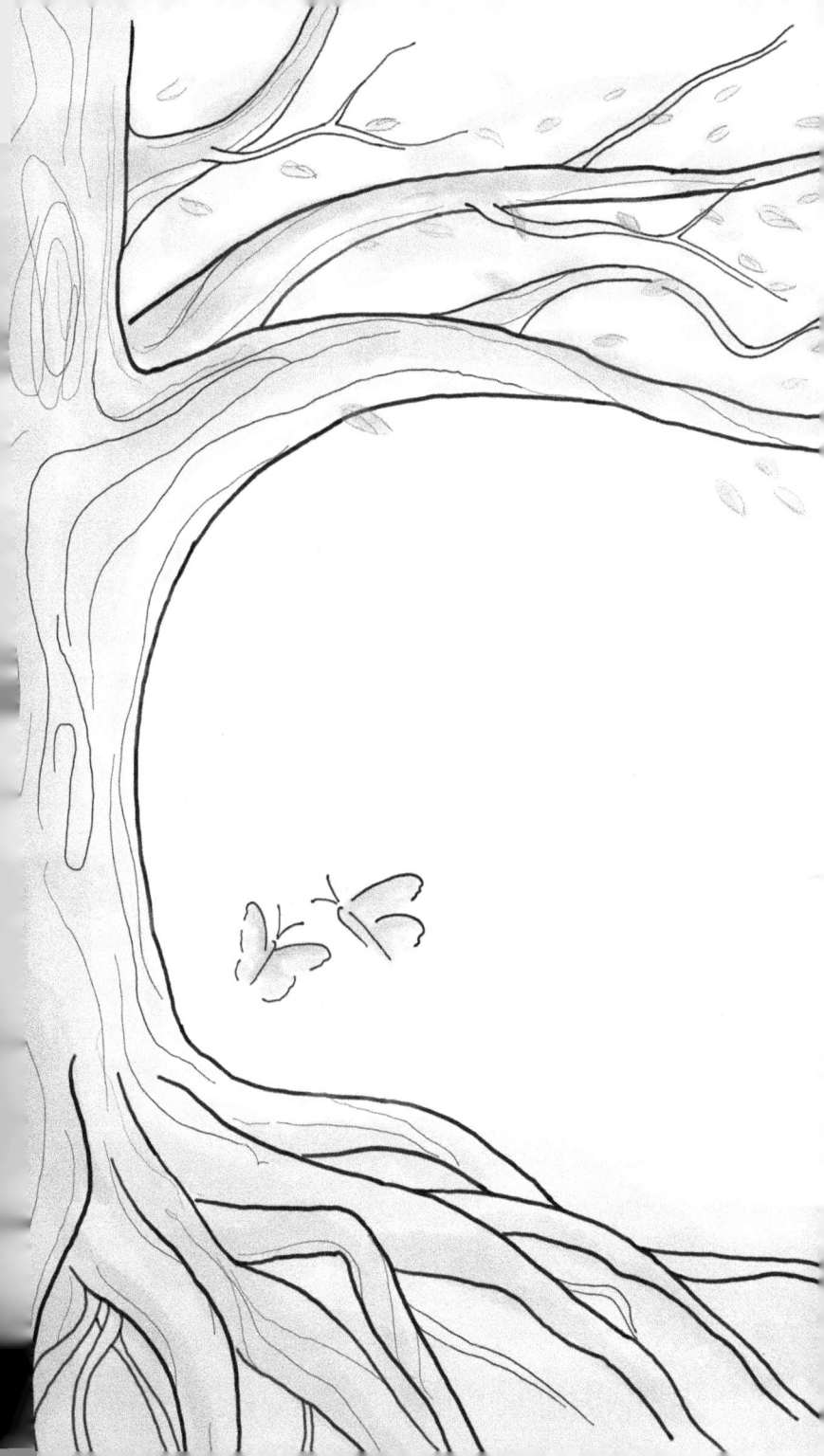

www.ingramcontent.com/pod-product-compliance
Lightning Source LLC
Chambersburg PA
CBHW022109090426
42743CB00008B/783